Cambridge El

Elements in Epist
edited by
Stephen Hetherington
University of New South Wales, Sydney

COHERENTISM

Erik J. Olsson
Lund University

CAMBRIDGE
UNIVERSITY PRESS

Shaftesbury Road, Cambridge CB2 8EA, United Kingdom

One Liberty Plaza, 20th Floor, New York, NY 10006, USA

477 Williamstown Road, Port Melbourne, VIC 3207, Australia

314–321, 3rd Floor, Plot 3, Splendor Forum, Jasola District Centre,
New Delhi – 110025, India

103 Penang Road, #05–06/07, Visioncrest Commercial, Singapore 238467

Cambridge University Press is part of Cambridge University Press & Assessment,
a department of the University of Cambridge.

We share the University's mission to contribute to society through the pursuit of
education, learning and research at the highest international levels of excellence.

www.cambridge.org
Information on this title: www.cambridge.org/9781009055123

DOI: 10.1017/9781009053327

First published 2022

A catalogue record for this publication is available from the British Library.

ISBN 978-1-009-05512-3 Paperback
ISSN 2398-0567 (online)
ISSN 2514-3832 (print)

Cambridge University Press & Assessment has no responsibility for the persistence
or accuracy of URLs for external or third-party internet websites referred to in this
publication and does not guarantee that any content on such websites is, or will
remain, accurate or appropriate.

Coherentism

Elements in Epistemology

DOI: 10.1017/9781009053327
First published online: September 2022

Erik J. Olsson
Lund University
Author for correspondence: Erik J. Olsson, erik_j.olsson@fil.lu.se

Abstract: Perhaps the most fundamental question of epistemology asks on what grounds our knowledge of the world ultimately rests. The traditional Cartesian answer is that it rests on indubitable facts arrived at through rational insight or introspection. Coherentists reject this answer, claiming instead that knowledge arises from relations of coherence or mutual support: if our beliefs cohere, we can be sure that they are mostly true. Sections 1 and 2 of this Element introduce the reader to the main ideas and problems of coherentism. Section 3 describes the "probabilistic turn," leading up to recent demonstrations that coherence fails to be conducive to truth. Sections 4 and 5 reassess the current debate about the proper definition of coherence from the standpoint of Rudolf Carnap's methodology of explication. The upshot is a tentative and qualified defense of one of the early coherence measures.

Keywords: coherentism, coherence theory, epistemology, knowledge, probability

ISBNs: 9781009055123 (PB), 9781009053327 (OC)
ISSNs: 2398-0567 (online), 2514-3832 (print)

Contents

1 Introduction

Perhaps the most fundamental question of epistemology asks on what grounds our knowledge of the world ultimately rests.[1] The traditional Cartesian answer is that it rests on indubitable facts arrived at through rational insight or introspection. Later authors have argued, in a more naturalistic spirit, that knowledge is rather due to causal connections from the world to the mind. Coherentists reject both these answers, claiming instead that the kind of justification required for knowledge arises from relations of coherence or mutual support between our beliefs. If our beliefs cohere, we can be sure that they are mostly true, at least under favorable conditions. Some even believe that coherence is what truth consists in, a position that is, for reasons that are well known, deeply problematic and will not be considered here.

Coherentism or, as it is also called, the coherence theory, long suffered from underdevelopment regarding the crucial concept of coherence, which was considered too vague to be of any epistemological use. In the 1990s, however, the theory experienced a probabilistic turn: several authors suggested defining and even measuring coherence by using the better-understood concept of probability. Unfortunately, this development led to a plethora of approaches without agreement on a particular account. This challenge is taken up in this Element. Rather than viewing coherence measures as conceptual analyses, they are construed here as explications or rational reconstructions. The question then becomes, not only how faithful they are to presystematic intuition, but also how epistemologically fruitful they prove to be.

Section 2 introduces the reader to the main ideas and problems of coherentism as an answer to the traditional questions of epistemology. Section 3 centers on the probabilistic turn, surveying 20 years of research on probabilistic coherence measures and their purported connections to truth and other desirable epistemic properties, leading up to the so-called impossibility results purporting to show – perhaps surprisingly – that coherence, no matter how the concept is made formally precise, cannot possibly be connected to truth, in fact, not even in a weak ceteris paribus sense and under favorable conditions. The state of the art is seen to consist of a plethora of different proposals for how to come to grips with the resulting paradox. Furthermore, quite independently of these results, the problem of finding an adequate definition of coherence remains largely unsolved as well. The final part, starting with Section 4,

---

[1] I am concerned here with our knowledge of the external world as opposed to our knowledge of mental states, mathematics, or logic.

reassesses the definitional debate from an explicationist standpoint and cul-
minates in a tentative and qualified defence of one of the early coherence
measures.[2]

2 Coherentism and the Problems of Epistemology – The Early Debate

2.1 The Promises of Coherentism

According to coherentism, our knowledge of the world ultimately rests on the
coherence or mutual support between our beliefs – beliefs that, taken singly,
need not be very probable, or, on some accounts, may even lack credence
altogether. The prima facie dialectical advantages of a coherentist position
should be clear.[3] Since it does not presuppose a foundation of indubitable truths,
it bypasses the traditional and seemingly never-ending empiricist–rationalist
controversy. Moreover, contrary to some forms of externalism, coherentism
seems to do better justice to our specifically *human* knowledge, which often
involves complex higher-order thought in ways that seem difficult to reduce to
world-belief causality. However, it is one thing to suggest a new epistemological framework and quite another to actually provide the necessary details. It
is at this point the coherentist faces a number of traditional challenges. For one,
while the guiding intuition behind foundationalism is quite clear – foundational
beliefs support other beliefs without themselves requiring any support – it is
considerably more difficult to understand how beliefs could mutually support
each other as the coherentist wants us to believe. Perhaps the most famous
attempt to make sense of this idea comes from Willard Van Orman Quine and
his web-of-belief metaphor (Quine and Ullian, 1970). Mutually supporting
beliefs form a structure much like a spider's web, it is suggested. Yet, even
a web needs to be anchored to something outside itself. For Quine, this anchor-
ing is provided by the external causal connection afforded by sensory stimula-
tion. Causality, however, is an externalist element that is unfortunately
unavailable to a strict coherentist. As one could imagine, proponents of coherentism have had various proposals for how to make sense of coherentism
without succumbing to externalism or (strong forms of) foundationalism.
Some of the more well-known attempts can be found in the works of Brand

---

[2] I would like to thank the anonymous reviewers for their criticism and valuable suggestions, which
led to many clarifications and other improvements, and my editor Stephen Hetherington for
inviting me to write a book on coherentism for the Cambridge Element series, and for his
professionalism during the publication process. My work on the Element was finalized while
I was a fellow at the Stellenbosch Institute of Advanced Studies (STIAS). I am grateful to STIAS
for providing excellent facilities and an inspiring intellectual environment.
[3] This section draws on chapter 7 in Olsson (2021a).

Blanshard (1939), A. C. Ewing (1934), C. I. Lewis (1946), Nicholas Rescher (1973), Donald Davidson (1986), Keith Lehrer (1990), Laurence Bonjour (1985), and Paul Thagard (2000).

On closer scrutiny, there are two (related) suggestions for how coherence could ground, explain, or justify all our knowledge, and we will consider them separately. First, coherence has been considered part of a solution to the traditional regress problem in epistemology. On the standard account of knowledge, often attributed to Plato, the fact that a person knows that p is to be analyzed as that person having a justified true belief that p, which is in turn taken to imply that the person has (sufficiently) good reasons for that belief. Now, those reasons in favor of p must presumably themselves be cases of knowledge, or the person's knowledge that p would rest on something less than knowledge (viz., on ignorance). That knowledge could rest on ignorance is uniformly dismissed as an absurd proposal. But then the same thing can be said of the reasons themselves: they too must rest on further knowledge, leading to an infinite regress of reasons for reasons, and so on. The upshot is known as the Agrippean trilemma: the reasons must either not end at all, end in foundational beliefs that are in some sense self-evident, or, alternatively, form a circular set of ultimately self-supporting elements, similar to the coherentists' notion of a web of belief. It is a trilemma, of course, because none of the three alternatives appears very attractive. As we will see in a moment, coherentists have argued that there are further options for how to deal with the regress, options that crucially involve the concept of coherence yet purport to avoid the obvious problems with the circular-reasons approach.

Moving on to the second problem, it is undoubtedly true that our knowledge of the world has to come from some source, be it observation, testimony, or something else. Furthermore, no such source of information arguably is completely reliable in itself, making the resulting report less than completely certain. Therefore, it is concluded, we can never attain the degree of certainty required for knowledge. Since we do think we have knowledge, this train of thought gives rise to a predicament that I will refer to as the uncertainty problem. The coherentist grants the premises of this argument yet argues that a sufficient level of certainty can still be obtained, provided that several sources are consulted and found to deliver coherent verdicts. This is the idea to which most of this book is devoted. Yet, before we examine it more closely, let us return to the regress problem and its proposed coherence solution.

There is an obvious objection to the "naïve" coherentist proposal that our reasons should move in circles, namely, that circular reasons are illegitimate in a rational debate. A solution to the regress problem, which legitimizes obviously irrational ways of reasoning, is unlikely to be met with much enthusiasm. To overcome this objection, Laurence BonJour (1985) proposed a more sophisticated theory. BonJour grants that a coherence theorist cannot allow circular reasoning. However, he does not think that this disqualifies a coherentist approach to the regress. Rather, the coherentist response must, he submits, free itself from the linear thinking behind the regress.

Specifically, the central elements of BonJour's theory are the following:

1. What is primarily justified is a person's entire system of beliefs, not individual beliefs within that system.
2. A system is justified if it is coherent.
3. Individual beliefs are justified and can constitute knowledge if they are part of such a justified system.

On this account, coherence plays the role of justifying the whole system of a person's beliefs, giving the person sufficient reasons to hold the totality of beliefs in the system to be true (at least in sufficient approximation). Individual beliefs are justified, moreover, if they are part of such a justified coherent system. Crucially, this account does not require that we accept circular reasons and thus avoids the previously mentioned objection to a naïve coherence theory. BonJour's proposal, however, so far leaves open how the notion of coherence should be defined more precisely. When is a system of beliefs (sufficiently) coherent? We return to this question in a moment. Before we do, let us quickly review the idea that coherence could figure in a solution to the second – uncertainty – problem.

In our everyday lives, we usually rely on the information that is available. This applies to both the information we receive from our senses – sight, hearing, taste, and so on – as well as that which we receive from other people, directly or indirectly through other media, radio, television, and, more recently, the Internet. Our trust in the information presented is, by default, automatic, as many philosophers in the American pragmatist tradition following C. S. Peirce have stressed. This is perhaps most evident regarding the testimony of the senses. My belief that John is sitting over there arises directly as the result of observing him. Thus, unlike what the earlier empiricists suggested, it is hardly the case that I first obtain an impression of John and then, after mature consideration, infer that he is actually there, or at least that would be a less usual situation. The same goes for what other people say. If my colleague says that Audrey is in her office, I normally take it for granted that her statement is true without reflecting on various more skeptical alternatives.

The fact that we incorporate much information in an unreflective manner does not mean, of course, that the underlying cognitive mechanism is completely uncritical. Testimonies from other people, for instance, are accepted only so long as there is no positive reason to believe that something has gone wrong. If there are explicit reasons to be vigilant, acceptance by default is disengaged and we enter a new, more skeptical mode of thinking. In Peirce's terminology, we have left the pleasant state of "belief" and entered a less satisfactory state of "doubt." One reason for such disengagement may be the perceived conflict between the information received from two different sources. There may also be explicit reasons to distrust our informant based on, say, a dubious track record. Is she in fact trying to mislead us the way she has done in the past?

So long as everything goes smoothly and we accept information automatically, we have no reason to think twice about the coherence or consistency between the information provided by our sources. Consulting a single source of information is enough to settle the question at hand. Considerations of coherence come into play only when there is reason to question our sources and the information they provide. In such cases, it may be of interest to listen to more than one report. If what multiple sources say shows a high degree of coherence – if their reports mutually support each other – we can, it seems, conclude that what they say is probably true, even if the sources are not very credible when considered individually.

To illustrate, suppose that a robbery has been committed and that the police are now questioning the witnesses. The first witness says that Bert was at the crime scene at the time of the robbery, the second that Bert owns a weapon of the type used, and the third that Bert shortly after the robbery transferred a large sum of money to his bank account. None of these items of information is particularly damaging on its own; after all, many people may have been at the crime scene, the gun may be a of a popular brand, and so on. Yet, taken together they may constitute a sufficient ground to incriminate Bert in connection with the robbery. In general, as many authors, some of whom we will soon encounter, have insisted, a high probability for a particular conclusion can be obtained by combining individually unimpressive reports, provided their coherence is significant.

What has been said so far is intended to illustrate how coherence can boost credibility in situations that, although not entirely normal in that the sources are in doubt, still are not too out of the ordinary. Although we cannot accept the information presented at face value, there is still background knowledge that we can appeal to, suggesting, for example, that most witnesses are not completely unreliable. The step seems short to claim that if coherence works so well when we are *almost* ignorant of the qualities of the sources, perhaps the effect is the same when we are *completely* ignorant thereof, in which case coherence would be the long-sought-for Holy Grail of epistemology that could forever silence even the most radical of skeptics.

What has been said so far leaves us with several pressing questions. Is the coherentist correct in her claims about coherence and its positive effects on probability? Does coherence really admit inference to high probability? If so, under what conditions does this occur? Above all, is the anti-skeptical use of coherence in the end convincing? The problems are difficult, and the space allotted to the present book is less than that required for a full examination. My modest aim will be to cover some of the more important advances in the field, beginning with the concept of coherence itself.

2.2 Defining Coherence – Some Early Attempts

An early attempt to give the concept of coherence a precise meaning can be found in the work of A. C. Ewing (1934).[4] According to Ewing, a coherent set of statements is characterized by freedom from contradiction as well as by the fact that each statement in the set follows logically from the other statements taken together. Thus, the set consisting of the statements p, q, and r is coherent according to Ewing if it does not contain a contradiction and if p follows logically from q and r, q follows logically from p and r, and, finally, r follows logically from p and q. This attempt to define coherence exclusively in terms of logical consequence is usually criticized for being too narrow in relation to our ordinary concept of coherence: many sets that we naturally judge to be coherent do not meet Ewing's requirements. Our earlier example with Bert illustrates this proposal's lack of appeal in relation to presystematic judgment:

p: "Bert was at the scene of the crime."
q: "Bert owns a weapon of the type used by the robber."
r: "Bert deposited a large sum of money in his account the following day."

No doubt, most people would judge this set of statements to be coherent: the statements are consistent and, to some extent, support each other. Yet, none of the statements follows with logical necessity from the combination of the others. For example, there is no logical contradiction in claiming that p and q are true, but that r is not: one can well imagine a situation where Bert was at the scene of the crime and owns a weapon of the relevant type but, nevertheless, did not deposit any money. It follows that the set, while coherent in an intuitive sense, is not coherent if Ewing's definition is used. In fact, it is difficult to find naturally occurring sets of statements that satisfy Ewing's austere main condition. Unsurprisingly, given his own restrictive account, Ewing ultimately held coherence to be too profound a concept to be captured in a formula.

---

[4] It is useful to distinguish epistemological inquiries into coherence before and after the "probabilistic turn" in the late 1990s. By "early attempts" I mean those belonging to the former.

C. I. Lewis's definition of what he called "congruence" is more promising (Lewis, 1946). Lewis introduced the term to mark his departure from the coherence theory of truth in which coherence is used to define rather than, as Lewis proposes, be indicative of truth. Thus, his intention was to use "congruence" as a technical term for coherence in the sense of mutual support (Lewis, 1946, p. 338). To avoid the multiplication of terms with a similar meaning, I will stick to "coherence" in the following. According to Lewis, a set is coherent just in case, in effect, every proposition in the set is supported by the other propositions taken together. So far, the definition is very similar to Ewing's, except that for Lewis being supported means something else than it does for Ewing. One proposition being supported by another means here that the probability of the former is increased if the latter is assumed to be true. The proposition "Donald contracts lung cancer" is, in this sense, supported by the proposition "Donald is a heavy smoker" because the probability of contracting lung cancer increases if it is assumed that the person is a heavy smoker. Since this is a less austere way of looking at support between propositions, Lewis's definition is broader than Ewing's in the sense that it, disregarding some special cases, makes more sets coherent than the latter.

Let us illustrate the difference between Ewing's and Lewis's accounts by returning to the Bert case. We saw that the set consisting of p, q, and r, though intuitively coherent, fails to be coherent according to Ewing's definition. This is not so if Lewis's definition is used instead. In the present case, the fact that Bert was at the crime scene and possesses a weapon of the right kind arguably increases the probability that he in fact committed the crime, which in turn increases the likelihood that he would deposit money in his account. The propositions p and q therefore together make r more likely. For similar reasons, p and r together make q more likely, and the same is true of q and r in relation to p. It is worth stressing that the propositions in a set that is coherent in Lewis's sense need not support each other very strongly; it is sufficient that they do so only slightly.

Moving on, BonJour presented his own account of coherence in his 1985 book. His definition is much more complicated and not as precise as Ewing's and Lewis's proposals. BonJour defends the increased complexity by reference to his intention to capture more aspects of the concept. Rather than providing an outright definition, he proposes the following coherence criteria (BonJour, 1985, pp. 95–99):

1. A system of beliefs is coherent only if it is logically consistent.
2. A system of beliefs is coherent in proportion to its degree of probabilistic consistency.

3. The coherence of a system of beliefs is increased by the presence of inferential connections between its component beliefs and increased in proportion to the number and strength of such connections.
4. The coherence of a system of beliefs is diminished to the extent to which it is divided into subsystems of beliefs that are relatively unconnected to each other by inferential connections.
5. The coherence of a system of beliefs is decreased in proportion to the presence of unexplained anomalies in the believed content of the system.

BonJour's coherence criteria relate coherence to several other concepts: logical and probabilistic consistency, inferential connections between beliefs, and the notion of anomaly. The first criterion is a familiar one that we encountered in Ewing's work. Regarding probabilistic consistency, the crucial concept in the second criterion, BonJour writes (1985, p. 95):

> Suppose that my system of beliefs contains both the belief that P and also the belief that it is extremely improbable that P. Clearly such a system of beliefs may perfectly well be logically consistent. But it is equally clear from an intuitive standpoint that a system which contains two such beliefs is significantly less coherent than it would be without them and thus that probabilistic consistency is a second factor determining coherence.

According to the second criterion, the situation just described should be avoided for as many beliefs as possible. The concept of an inference connection, which appears in the third and fourth criteria, should be interpreted broadly to include all types of support relations between propositions or beliefs, including logical and probabilistic support.

According to the fourth criterion, systems consisting of independent, inferentially unconnected parts score relatively low on coherence. An extreme case would be a person suffering from split personality, but there are, of course, less spectacular examples of belief systems affected by fragmentation. For example, a child can learn all about cats and all about dogs without considering what these animal species have in common, so that one part of the child's belief system is about cats and another, distinct part about dogs. In time, the child acquires the concept of mammal and comes to understand that much of what is true of cats and dogs comprises general features of mammals. In science, it is not uncommon for two areas previously regarded as separate fields to become connected through unification, that is, the discovery that they are special cases of a more general theory (cf. Friedman, 1974). As in the case of the child, such a development is to be welcomed, BonJour submits, because it increases the coherence of the overall system. I will return to the topic of coherence as unification in Section 5.5. BonJour's last criterion states that the occurrence of anomalies has negative impact as far as coherence is concerned. Roughly, an anomaly is an observational belief that cannot be explained within the belief system in question.

There are many issues with BonJour's theory that I cannot discuss in detail here. A general difficulty with theories that view coherence as a multifaceted concept is explaining how the different aspects interact. It may well be that a system *S* is more coherent than another system *T* in one respect, but that *T* is more coherent than *S* in another. For example, *S* may score higher regarding inferential connections, but also contain more anomalies, than *T*. In such a case, the second criterion implies that *S* is more coherent than *T*, whereas the fifth criterion suggests the opposite. On a charitable interpretation, the criteria should be seen as ceteris paribus conditions stating what is more coherent, *everything else being equal*; they do not determine whether one system is more coherent than another in a general sense.

A more exact and systematic account of coherence, which emphasizes the role of explanation in coherence, has been presented by Paul Thagard in numerous articles and books, starting with Thagard (1989). His "principles of explanatory coherence" in Thagard (2000), p. 43, are stated as follows:

Principle E1 (Symmetry) Explanatory coherence is a symmetric relation, unlike, say, conditional probability. That is, two propositions A and B cohere with each other equally.

Principle E2 (Explanation) a. A hypothesis coheres with what it explains, which can be either evidence or another hypothesis. b. Hypotheses that together explain some other proposition cohere with each other. c. The more hypotheses it takes to explain something, the lower the degree of coherence.

Principle E3 (Analogy) Similar hypotheses that explain similar pieces of evidence cohere.

Principle E4 (Data Priority) Propositions that describe the results of observation have a degree of acceptability on their own.

Principle E5 (Contradiction) Contradictory propositions are incoherent with each other.

Principle E6 (Competition) If A and B both explain a proposition, and if A and B are not explanatorily connected, then A and B are incoherent with each other. (A and B are explanatorily connected if one explains the other or if together they explain something.)

Principle E7 (Acceptance) The acceptability of a proposition in a system of propositions depends on its coherence with them.[5]

Like BonJour's criteria, Thagard's principles do not provide an outright definition of coherence. Rather, his principles serve to constrain the meaning of the term, for example by stipulation that contradictory propositions are incoherent with each other (*E5*). Presumably, the principles can be satisfied by quite different, more-specific accounts of the central concepts. In fact, Thagard's principles do not only constrain the meaning of coherence; they also constrain the circumstances under which propositions are acceptable. Thus, *E4* states that observational propositions have a degree of acceptability on their own, and *E7* that the acceptability of a proposition in a system depends on its coherence with other propositions in the system. Again, these are constraints and not definitions. Principle *E4*, furthermore, is interesting because it reveals that Thagard's theory is not a pure coherence theory but rather a kind of weak foundationalism (along the lines of C. I. Lewis; see Section 2.3). Thagard has implemented *E1* to *E7* in different formal frameworks, such as neural network theory, including algorithms for determining a set of accepted propositions in accordance with *E7* (cf. section 2.3 in Thagard, 2000).

2.3 Coherence and Truth

To what extent is coherence relevant for determining the truthfulness of a system of statements? Can we, for instance, infer the truth of the statements from their coherence? The notion that the relationship between truth and coherence would be of this simple kind has been criticized from several perspectives. The most important critique – the so-called isolation objection – reminds us that a system can be highly or even maximally coherent without have anything whatsoever to do with reality. A dream can be highly coherent without being a reflection of fact. The fact that Inspector Wallander dreamed that Bert was at a crime scene, owns a weapon of the right kind, and deposited money the day after does not make it likely that these propositions are true, despite the fact that we already noted that these propositions form a coherent set, intuitively as well as in Lewis's sense. The situation is different if the information comes from several witnesses, one saying that Bert was at the scene of the crime, the other that he owns the gun, and so on. In that case, we are likely to accept the testimonies as credible. This salient difference between the dream

---

[5] Thagard's account raises a number of issues, such as how we individuate hypotheses, what "degree of acceptability" means, what is entailed by saying that two hypotheses are "explanatorily connected," and so on. For an extensive critical discussion of Thagard's theory, see Olsson (2005), section 9.4.

and the witness scenario cannot lie in the coherence of the propositions, which is the same in both cases. What is it, then, that makes the coherence significant in the witness but not in the dream scenario? It is useful to consider this question by referring to the early debate in the works of C. I. Lewis and Laurence BonJour supplemented with a few additional observations that I believe have strong support in common sense. As we will see in the next section, the correctness of the view presented here has been, in the view of most informed observers, rigorously demonstrated within probability theory.

Now, there are two salient differences between the witness and the dream scenario. In the former, we can assume that each individual witness is at least somewhat reliable. There are, to be sure, witnesses who deliberately lie or for other reasons speak untruthfully, but most are probably worthy of some trust. As C. A. J. Coady famously argued, the general unreliability of human testimony is plausibly not even a conceptual possibility (Coady, 1992; see also section 5.3 in Olsson, 2005). In the absence of reasons to believe otherwise, we can therefore assume that a witness about whom we lack specific information is not completely unreliable. If such a witness says that Bert was at the scene of the crime, this is some small reason to believe that he was indeed there. On the other hand, there is not much more we can say unless we have additional information about the witness (for example, through another character witness), as it would be gullible to consider every witness one comes across highly reliable. The point is that we lack any corresponding reason to assume that the different parts of a dream were formed in a way that reliably tracks the facts of the matter. The fact that Wallander dreamt that Bert was at a crime scene gives us not the faintest of reasons to think that Bert was indeed there.

The second salient difference has to do with the degree of independence in the two cases. If we consult several witnesses, we may often assume that they are independent so long as there is no evidence to the contrary. Exactly how the concept of independence should be understood will be clearer in the next section. What we can say already at this point is that independence is normally present when the witnesses have not spoken to, or otherwise influenced, each other prior to giving their testimonies. If, by contrast, they secretly met beforehand and agreed to incriminate Bert, they cannot be considered independent. While testimonies can normally be assumed to be independent, this is not the case for the various elements of a dream. There is no reason to believe that the individual constituents of Wallander's dream about Bert would, in the same sense, have arisen independently. He may well have dreamed that Bert went to the bank just because he had previously dreamed that Bert was at the scene of the crime. The dream may have created its own coherence, as it were.[6]

What we have isolated are two factors that characterize the circumstances under which coherence has any effect on what we perceive to be probable: sources need to be not only individually somewhat reliable and their reports correspondingly credible, but also collectively independent. The question is whether both are needed or whether it is sufficient that one factor is present but not the other. Suppose that the witnesses are partially reliable but not independent. Such a situation would arise if one of the witnesses, Peter, say, is partially reliable and has, perhaps at gunpoint, influenced the others to repeat his own testimony. It goes without saying that in such a case the evidential value of the joint testimonies does not exceed the evidential value of Peter's singular report. Since the other testimonies can be discarded as irrelevant, the question of their coherence does not even arise. Of course, this would be an extreme case of complete lack of independence. Common sense dictates that just a tiny bit of dependence hardly prohibits coherence from having a beneficial effect on probability, although we would expect that effect to be lower than it would have been had the sources been entirely independent.

Suppose, conversely, that the witnesses are collectively independent but individually completely unreliable. We can imagine, for example, that we hear several independent witnesses, all of whom were too far away from the scene of the crime to have seen anything more specific. Suppose that they nevertheless give the same testimony: the perpetrator was a blond man wearing a black leather jacket, say. How would we react in such a situation? If, as we have assumed, the witnesses were indeed too far away, we would supposedly view the fact of coherence as a curious coincidence explained entirely by chance. In this case, too, the fact that the witnesses give coherent accounts has no influence on the probability that what they claim is true.

It should be added that the observation that the witnesses independently agree on something rather specific, despite being assumed to be completely unreliable, may be perceived as an anomaly, much in BonJour's sense: the observation of an event so unlikely that it requires an explanation beyond chance. Indeed, given independence and complete unreliability, it is highly unlikely that the witnesses, if they are many, would concur on any particular detail. An anomaly may be a reason to reconsider our current assumptions, including those about the unreliability and independence of witnesses.

---

[6] The same is true, to a lesser extent, of memories. Coherence may enter as a causal factor in the production of what we seem to remember. See Olsson (2017b) for this point. See also Section 2.4.

In conclusion, the coherence of a set of statements constitutes a reason to believe that the statements in the set are true, provided that the sources of information are partially reliable and collectively independent. Both these favorable circumstances must normally be met for coherence to have a positive effect. This still does not mean, however, that the probability of truth will exceed the threshold required for certainty and knowledge. Even so, a very high probability can be attained in this way even if the sources are only slightly reliable. Every else being equal, adding more sources that give coherent verdicts will increase the probability of truth to the point at which it is arbitrarily close to 1. Yet, absolute certainty is thereby not attained but at best the practical certainty that the British empiricist John Locke thought was the most we can hope to achieve in our daily affairs. Even so, the justification traditionally required for knowledge may very well be of a coherentist kind: a person's main reasons for claiming to know may refer to multiple sources reporting the proposition in question to be true.

The precise probability attained through coherence in favorable circumstances intuitively depends on two things. First, it depends on how reliable the sources are individually. If the sources are relatively reliable, relatively few coherent reports are required to attain a given level of probability. Second, it also depends on the prior probability of what is reported. If what was said was already relatively likely, comparatively few coherent reports are required for the attainment of a high probability. There are some caveats here, though: there are important cases where a relatively low initial probability leads, counterintuitively, to a relatively high probability after the coherence is observed.[7] At any rate, the following applies in general: in order to give a more precise estimate of the probability attained in a particular case, more is required than the observation that the sources are somewhat reliable and independent; it is also necessary to have information about how reliable they are, and how likely the reported propositions were before they were reported. These observations will be important when we return to the anti-skeptical application of coherence reasoning.

2.4 Coherence as an Answer to the Radical Skeptic

I now return to the uncertainty problem identified in Section 2.1. The kind of skepticism that I am interested in states that all we can know directly is of a report nature, a common enough view in traditional epistemology (e.g., Chisholm, 1977).[8] What we can know directly is that our senses, our memory,

---

[7] For this point, see Olsson (2002a), and for further discussion Boven, Fitelson, Hartmann, and Snyder (2002) and Olsson (2002b).

[8] This section summarizes the criticism of coherentism in Olsson (2002c) and, in greater detail, Olsson (2005).

and so forth report that such and such is the case; we cannot know that things really are as they indicate. Thus, I can know directly that I seem to see John, that is, that my faculty of observation reports that John is standing in front of me, not that John is in fact there. Similarly, I can know directly that I seem to recall that as a child I received many Christmas presents, that is, that my memory reports this, not that I in fact received many presents. The same applies to our current beliefs. All we can know directly is that we have those beliefs, that our belief system "reports" that we have them, not that the propositions thus believed are true.[9]

The coherence objection to this form of skepticism, as I mentioned, states that we can attain knowledge that our beliefs are true if the propositions reported form a coherent set. This is the basic idea behind C. I. Lewis's justification of the faculty of memory, the proposal being that a person can justify her memories by reference to their degree of coherence. Suppose you (seem to) remember not only that you used to get many Christmas presents as a child but also that the whole family used to gather to celebrate Christmas. These two (seeming) memories are coherent: the more relatives, the more Christmas presents for the children; and the more Christmas presents, the more relatives were presumably there. Let us further assume that most of your (seeming) memories exhibit such mutual support. According to the coherence proposal, this means that you can be practically certain that what you remember actually happened.

But here we have to be careful: as we saw, coherence has a positive effect on the probability of contents of reports only if the reports are partially credible and independent. In particular, in order to infer the truth of seeming memories from the coherence of their contents, we must know that they are partially credible and independent – or at least be able rationally to assume this. This may not be impossible in principle if the seeming memories whose coherence we are interested in belong to someone else, that is, if we consider another person's memory reports from our own third-person perspective. For it is not problematic in principle to assume that the other person's memories are generally partially credible and independent and, if so, to infer from our observation of coherence that the memories are by and large true. But this would be a kind of externalist coherence theory that is, for reasons already mentioned, traditionally considered irrelevant to the problem at hand. The hope of the coherentist approach is rather that a person should be able to conclude that *her own* memories are highly probable from observing the considerable degree to which they cohere. However, this presupposes that the person can know or rationally assume that *her own* memories are partially reliable and independent.

---

[9] Cf. the discussion of the "doxastic presumption" in BonJour (1985).

The problem is that, in the present dialectical context, any appeal to her memories – including remembrances of the percentage of cases in which they reliably recorded facts – would be disallowed, on pain of vicious circularity.

The problem becomes even more severe if what the person is trying to justify from her first-person perspective is not her memories but her empirical beliefs. For the observation that the system of her beliefs is highly coherent to imply that the beliefs are largely true, the person must justifiably believe that her beliefs are partially credible and independent. But since the latter beliefs are plausibly of an empirical nature, this means that they are part of the very system whose truth is at stake. We recall our granted assumption that the person does not have direct knowledge of the contents of her own beliefs but only of their existence as such. Thus, the person cannot assume in the process of justifying all her empirical beliefs that her de facto beliefs about partial credibility and independence are true. It now follows that, as a matter of principle, a person cannot, from her own perspective, justify the totality of her own beliefs by appeal to coherence.

The only way out for the anti-skeptic seems to be to argue that our beliefs about the partial credibility and independence of our empirical memories or beliefs are themselves not justified empirically but justified a priori. Regarding credibility, it could be argued that reason would break down completely without this assumption firmly in place. So dependent are we on memory that it is difficult even to imagine a life without its guidance. Perhaps, we must assume that our memories are generally to be trusted to function rationally at all. Indeed, Lewis (1946) argued that assigning some initial credibility to our seeming memories is a condition for the possibility of rational thought and action. Yet it should be clear that, even if this dialectical move succeeds, it remains to argue that our memories also exhibit a sufficient degree of independence, or any appeal to coherence will be of little value, a crucial point on which Lewis was, unfortunately, silent.[10] Again, the prospects are not brighter if what is to be justified are not our memories but our beliefs.

To make matters worse, even if the anti-skeptic were to succeed in these considerable feats, two further difficulties would still remain. C. I. Lewis's argument can at best show that we must assign positive credibility to our memories as such without implying anything definite about the degree of credibility thus assigned. Yet as we observed, we need more specific information in this regard to be able to assess, at least in approximation, the probability attained by combining coherent memories. Otherwise, we cannot satisfy ourselves that the probability is high enough to warrant practical certainty. As we

---

[10] The notion that our memories are generally independent is firmly rejected by cognitive psychology, which considers coherence to be, in important cases, a causal factor in the production of the seemingly remembered (cf. Olsson, 2017b).

also noted, we need in addition information regarding the prior probability of memory contents, namely the probability of the propositions remembered before they were mnemonically archived. When all these considerations are combined, the inevitable conclusion is that the coherentist's response to the skeptic has not only been so far unsuccessful, but that it is doomed to fail.

2.5 Coherence and Abduction

In the light of these serious problems, coherentism hardly offers a satisfactory answer to the classical problems of skepticism, whether or not the latter concerns memory, beliefs, or our trust in the statements of others. But that does not by any means imply that the concept of coherence itself is without value in everyday contexts. In our daily affairs, we put some trust in information because it is coherent with other information, and we do so for good reason: we know, or have reason to believe or assume, that the sources providing the information are at least somewhat reliable and independent. Furthermore, we have at least a hunch about how reliable the sources are and how likely the reported information was before it was reported.

But even in practical matters, we must concede that coherence itself is rarely enough to declare the end of inquiry, especially if the matter is important and stakes are high. In a legal context, for instance, we are reluctant to convict someone of a serious crime on purely circumstantial evidence, that is on the basis of a coherent body of alleged facts. The role of coherence is rather to point to interesting hypotheses that may be worthy of further investigation. Coherence is above all a factor to be reckoned with regarding what Peirce called abduction, the process by which plausible theories are selected for further testing.

The example with Bert may, once again, serve as an illustration. The three pieces of coherent information provided by the witnesses concerning Bert's whereabouts, his possessing a similar gun and his depositing of money, respectively, would normally not suffice for a conviction. However, they undeniably lead our suspicion in the direction of Bert. It would be reasonable, in the light of the coherent set of reports, to focus the investigation on the hypothesis that Bert did it. The next step would be to make a ballistic test of Bert's weapon, compare his DNA with that found at the crime scene, and so on, for the purposes of either confirming or disconfirming the hypothesis in question.

Based on these considerations, we can reformulate our criticism of the anti-skeptical use of the coherence theory in the following terms. Reference to the high degree of coherence of the totality of our own memories or beliefs could at best point to their actual truth being an interesting hypothesis for systematic inquiry. But this is as far as we get, since any attempt to verify the hypothesis would be challenged by a truly radical skeptic, who, by her very nature, does not accept any substantial empirical evidence at face value.

3 The Probabilistic Turn in Coherentist Epistemology

My criticism so far of the coherentist answer to radical skepticism, in Section 2, has been based on philosophical considerations that arguably qualify as sophisticated common sense, and I made no attempt to prove the conclusions reached with mathematical precision. In so far, the level of exactness did not saliently exceed that characterizing the works of C. I. Lewis and Laurence BonJour. What happened in the late 1990s, however, was that a number of researchers with a formal bent, including myself, became interested in the mathematical side of coherentism. Seminal articles are Huemer (1997) and Shogenji (1999), followed by Cross (1999), Bovens and Olsson (2000), and Olsson (2001). The effect of these investigations was that much of the criticism leveled in Section 2 against the anti-skeptical use of coherence could be formally underpinned, but also that new insights into coherence and truth were gained that, due to the complexity and delicacy of the reasoning involved, would have been difficult or even impossible to reach without employment of the proper mathematical tools. For most of these researchers, probability theory has been the formal framework of choice, which is why one can legitimately speak of a probabilistic turn in coherentist epistemology that coincided with the turn of the century.

As in the earlier coherentist literature, two problems motivated most of this work. I will refer to them as the *truth problem* and the *definition problem*, respectively. The truth problem consists in identifying the circumstances, if any, in which coherence is a sign of truth. The definition problem amounts to answering the question whether the concept of coherence can be precisely defined. As a first step, the central concepts, not least the concept of coherence itself, needed to be defined in the language of probability. Once this task had been accomplished, a formal investigation of the central coherentist claims could proceed. This methodology promised not only increased precision and objectivity, but also potential systematic advantages arising from interdisciplinary connections, including the transfer of concepts and results from areas in which probability theory had already proved its worth.

3.1 The Final Solution to the Truth Problem

The starting point for the probabilistic investigation of the truth problem was a specific controversy between Lewis and BonJour that seemed amenable to mathematical treatment. According to Lewis's position, often referred to as weak foundationalism, coherence raises the probability of a set of reported propositions only if the individual reports have some credibility in themselves, given that the reports are independent. In Lewis's own words (Lewis, 1946, p. 346):

> For any one of these reports, taken singly, the extent to which it confirms what is reported may be slight. And antecedently, the probability of what is reported may also be small. But congruence [which is Lewis's word for coherence] of the reports establishes a high probability of what they agree upon, by principles of probability determination which are familiar: on any other hypothesis than that of truth-telling, this agreement is highly unlikely; the story any one false witness might tell being one out of so very large a number of equally possible choices.

This is a view for which I found considerable intuitive support in Section 2. In his 1985 book, BonJour, however, rejects this element of Lewis's account, arguing instead that coherence can raise the probability of a set of reported propositions, given independence, even if the individual reports have no credibility in themselves but are in effect entirely without merit (BonJour, 1985, p. 148):

> What Lewis does not see, however, is that his own example shows quite convincingly that no antecedent degree of warrant or credibility is required. For as long as we are confident that the reports of the various witnesses are genuinely independent of each other, a high enough degree of coherence among them will eventually dictate the hypothesis of truth-telling as the only available explanation of their agreement – even, indeed, if those individual reports initially have a high degree of negative credibility, that is, are more likely to be false than true (for example, in the case where all of the witnesses are known to be habitual liars). And by the same token, so long as apparently cognitively spontaneous beliefs are genuinely independent of each other, their agreement will eventually generate credibility, without the need for an initial degree of warrant.

I dismissed this view in Section 2 on philosophical grounds, which may, of course, be questioned by someone with a different philosophical outlook. This move would be more difficult if Lewis could be proved right using mathematical reasoning in a standard framework such as probability theory.

One key concept here is the *probability of a set of reported propositions*, bearing in mind that "reported" can mean not only reported by witnesses or the like, but also, more abstractly, reported by the faculties of memory or belief. This concept is naturally formalized as a conditional probability, namely, the joint probability (the probability of the conjunction) of the propositions, given that they have been reported. Let $p_1, \ldots, p_n$ be the propositions in question and let $r_1, \ldots, r_n$ be the respective reports to the effect that the former are true. Then the probability in question can be expressed as

$$P(p_1 \wedge \ldots \wedge p_n | r_1, \ldots, r_n)^{11}.$$

In the case with Bert, for example, the reported propositions are p, q, and r – Bert being at the crime scene, owning a gun and depositing cash, respectively. We can let w_1, w_2, and w_3 stand for these propositions having been reported by witnesses 1, 2, and 3, respectively, in which case the relevant probability is

$$P(p \wedge q \wedge r | w_1, w_2, w_3).$$

We also need to formalize the concept of an *individual report being credible*. Again, probability theory suggests a natural definition, namely, the report being positively relevant to the proposition reported:

$$P(p_1 | r_1) > P(p_1).$$

Hence, an individual report is credible just in case it increases the probability of the proposition reported.[12]

The more intricate question is how to define *independence of reports* in probabilistic terms. Even so, this question, too, turns out to have a straightforward answer – and here the interdisciplinary connections I alluded to prove valuable. We recall the intuition that reports are independent to the extent that the reporters have not talked to or otherwise influenced each other before their reports were delivered. In the field of Artificial Intelligence, there is a whole subdiscipline devoted to applications in which statistical variables can be assumed independent in the present sense, namely the sub-discipline devoted to the study of Bayesian networks (Pearl, 1988). The way independence is defined there can be directly transferred to coherentist

---

[11] In their criticism of coherentism, Klein and Warfield (1994) misconstrue this probability as simply the joint probability of the reported propositions, $P(p_1 \wedge \ldots \wedge p_n)$, without conditionalizing on the fact that they have been reported (in their case reported as beliefs), as pointed out in Olsson (2001) and further elaborated in Bovens and Olsson (2002). See also Cross (1999) for a similar point.

[12] This is the sense in which a report is credible if it has some, however small, positive impact on the proposition in question. There is also a stronger notion of credibility according to which a report to be credible must raise the probability of the proposition above 0.5. See Olsson (2005), p. 65, footnote 4, for a discussion of why the present sense is the most relevant one for the purposes of the coherence theory. The matter is also touched upon in Olsson (2021b), section 5.

epistemology (cf. Bovens and Olsson, 2000). Suppose, to develop the Bert case, that both Karen and Maria report that Bert had a motive to commit the robbery. Assuming Karen's and Maria's reports to be individually credible, there is a trivial sense in which the reports will be dependent: a reliable witness reporting a proposition increases the probability of that proposition, which in turn increases the probability that the next reliable witness will report it as well. But this sort of dependence does not make Karen and Maria dependent in the relevant sense. Rather, what we are after is a sense of independence that does not, as it were, pass via the proposition reported. In other words, two reports are relevantly independent when they do not influence each other once the trivial kind of dependence just identified has been eliminated. Now, the trick to eliminate the trivial kind of dependence is to assume the reported proposition to have a definite truth value: true or false. This move "screens off" the reports from each other, in the sense that it precludes one report from influencing the other simply by raising the probability of the reported proposition.

Formally, letting m stand for Bert having a motive and r_1 and r_2 for Karin and Maria reporting this, respectively, their reports are independent just in case the following conditions hold:

(1) $P(r_2|m, r_1) = P(r_2|m)$

(2) $P(r_2|\neg m, r_1) = P(r_2|\neg m)$

The first clause states that Karen's report does not raise the probability of Maria's report, assuming that Bert had a motive. The second clause states that Karen's report does not raise the probability of Maria's report, assuming that Bert did not have a motive. A more general definition is possible but would lead us too far away from the philosophical points I am trying to make (see Olsson, 2002c).

The following can now be proved to hold:

Theorem (Olsson, 2002c): Independent reports that individually lack credibility leave the probability of the reported set of propositions unaffected.[13]

In other words, individually useless reports that are collectively independent do nothing for the probability of the reported propositions. This simple, yet fundamental, result has two important epistemological consequences. First, it bypasses the debate about the proper definition of coherence, holding regardless of what coherence means more precisely. Second, the theorem implies that however it is defined, coherence is not a sign of truth

---

[13] See Huemer (1997) for a similar, but less general, formal result.

if the independent reports lack individual credibility. Lewis was essentially right and BonJour wrong in this regard.[14] Coherentism, in its purest form, must be rejected. Every coherence theory must recognize a weak foundation of beliefs that have some credibility in themselves. Coherence cannot create credibility from scratch; it can at best amplify credibility already there.

3.2 The Impossibility of Truth-Conducive Measures of Coherence

Armed with the resources of probability theory, we can return to the second fundamental question: can the concept of coherence be given a precise definition? Again, the discussion can be framed, reasonably, as a contrast between two influential views. Whereas Ewing (1934), as we saw, ultimately held coherence to be too profound a concept to be captured in a formula, Lewis (1946) did not express similar doubts.

Once more, we need to make the question more precise before we can hope to find a compelling answer. Where Lewis defined coherence as a matter of all or nothing, contemporary researchers have found it more useful to conceive of coherence as a more fine-grained concept, admitting of (nontrivial) degrees. As a first approximation, such coherence measures assign each set of propositions a real number representing the degree of coherence of the set. Furthermore, since the very purpose of coherence is to be indicative of truth, the natural focus has been on the possibility of defining a coherence measure that is *truth-conducive*, namely that is such that a higher degree of coherence implies a higher probability of the reported propositions, the most basic question being whether there are such truth-conducive measures. Because of the theorem in the previous section, we need to add that the background conditions must involve reports that, besides being collectively independent, are also individually credible; else, no measure can be truth-conducive already for the reasons noted in the theorem. I will refer to these two favorable conditions as *Lewis conditions*.

The key concepts to be defined are *coherence measure* and *truth-conduciveness*. For the purposes of the present discussion, it will prove useful to define "coherence measure" in very broad terms. By a coherence measure, I will mean any function that assigns a real number to a set of (reported) propositions based on the probability of those propositions and possibly their negations and Boolean combinations (basically "and" and "or"). To illustrate,

---

[14] I wrote "essentially right" because, on closer scrutiny, Lewis's own definition of independent reports is weaker than the modern concept of conditional independence and, ironically, does not allow for the theorem to be proved. See Olsson (2005), section 3.5, for this point.

the first measure was proposed by Tomoji Shogenji (1999). It defines the coherence of a propositional set as the probability of the conjunction of the propositions divided by the product of their individual probabilities. For the case of two propositions:

$$C_{sho}(p,q) = \frac{P(p \wedge q)}{P(p) * P(q)}.$$

Shogenji suggested a straightforward generalization for the case of a finite set of propositions:

$$C_{sho}(p_1, \ldots, p_n) = \frac{P(p_1 \wedge \ldots \wedge p_n)}{P(p_1) * \ldots * P(p_n)}.$$

The next coherence measure to appear in the literature was proposed independently by David Glass (2002) and myself (Olsson, 2002c), as an extrapolation of a proposal in Bovens and Olsson (2000) to the effect that more agreement implies more coherence ceteris paribus (Figure 1). The ceteris paribus clause guarantees that the probability of the agreeing propositions remains the same.

Given the condition suggested by Bovens and myself, it is natural to go one step further and define agreement between propositions in terms of how much they overlap, that is, as the probability that they are all true (the probability of the conjunction) divided by the probability that either is (the probability of the disjunction). The resulting measure is sometimes called the "relative overlap," "Olsson," "Olsson–Glass,"or "Glass–Olsson" measure. I will use the latter label. For the case of two propositions,

$$C_{go}(p,q) = \frac{P(p \wedge q)}{P(p \vee q)}.$$

Both Glass and I suggested the following natural generalization for the case of a finite number of propositions:

$$C_{go}(p_1, \ldots, p_n) = \frac{P(p_1 \wedge \ldots \wedge p_n)}{P(p_1 \vee \ldots \vee p_n)}.$$

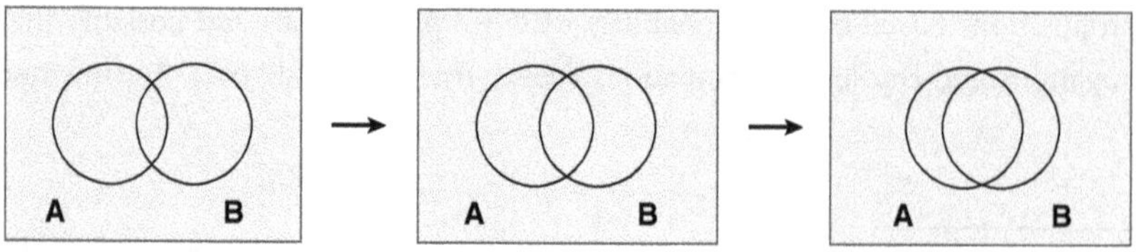

Figure 1 Progressively greater coherence due to increased overlap (Bovens and Olsson, 2000).

It is interesting to compare these two measures in some simple cases. In the extreme case of completely overlapping (equivalent) propositions, the Glass–Olsson measure takes on its maximum value, namely 1. This is so regardless of how probable the propositions are individually. This is not so for the Shogenji measure, which is sensitive to the individual probabilities even in the case of completely overlapping propositions. Specifically, complete agreement on something unlikely gives rise to higher coherence in the sense of the Shogenji measure. The latter is also sensitive to the number of agreeing propositions in a way in which the Glass–Olsson measure is not. On the former, but not on the latter, complete agreement by the many gives rise to higher coherence than complete agreement by the few. A high Glass–Olsson coherence means that the propositions in the set are close to being equivalent. Equivalent propositions are either all true or all false. Thus, a high Glass–Olsson coherence means, intuitively, that the propositions stand and fall together.

While a large number of measures have been proposed and studied in the literature since the appearance of the Shogenji and Glass–Olsson measures, many of which are quite complex, they remain the most discussed ones in recent works. As I will attempt to show in Section 5, they are not only strikingly simple, but also surprisingly fruitful, epistemically speaking.

Let us move on to the concept of truth-conduciveness. Besides what has already been said, we need to add one further element to its definition, namely, a ceteris paribus clause. As we noted in Section 2, the final probability of a set of reported propositions will be dependent on the degree to which the reports are credible. Thus, the degree of credibility needs to be held fixed when we study the effect of varying the coherence on the probability of the propositions in question.

Now, the question is whether there are coherence measures that are truth-conducive ceteris paribus under the Lewis conditions (Olsson, 2002c). In fact, there are no such measures:

Impossibility theorem (simplified): there are no coherence measures that are truth-conducive ceteris paribus under the Lewis conditions.

Bovens and Hartmann (2003) were the first to prove a theorem of this kind. A similar result by myself, in a different setting, appeared in Olsson (2005). The setting I studied involves a model in which there is uncertainty as to whether the reporters are perfectly reliable, in the sense of invariably telling the truth, or entirely unreliable, in which case they are no better than chance, but we can assign a probability to either possibility. (I will return to this model, and how it connects to Lewis's work, in the next section.) The model was proposed in Olsson (2002a), where I noted that the probability of a set of propositions varies in complex, yet predictable, ways with the probability of reliability. The central point in Olsson (2005) is roughly that, given two sets of propositions A and B, where A is more coherent than B according to a given coherence measure, we can always choose the probability of reliability strategically to obtain a situation in which B is, nonetheless, more probable than A, and still have the ceteris paribus condition and the Lewis conditions satisfied. Such a situation represents a counterexample to the truth-conduciveness of any given coherence measure. Given the way I tied the adequacy of a definition of a coherence measure to the potential of the latter to be truth-conducive in Olsson (2005), it follows that the concept of coherence is undefinable, which is indeed one of the central theses in that book and amounts to a modern way of saying that Ewing was right, or at least closer to the truth, than was Lewis.[15]

3.3 Beyond Truth-Conduciveness

The results presented here in response to the truth and definition problems are based on precise interpretations of presystematic concepts, such as "coherence," "independence," "credible reports," and so on. In principle, it is always possible to question formal interpretations of informal concepts. Formalization of pre-systematic concepts is an art and not an exact science. If the challenge is successful, a shadow of doubt also falls upon the results.

Most commentators who accept the probabilistic framework as suitable for the study of coherence have thought that the truth problem has thereby been solved, to the pure coherentist's disadvantage.[16] In contrast, the preceding approach to the definition problem has been challenged by several authors. A common criticism focuses on the requirement that an interesting coherence measure be truth-conducive in the specified sense. For instance, Bovens and Hartmann (2003) impose the requirement only in a restricted sense, that is, for propositional sets that they think are genuinely comparable, arguing that this condition is not satisfied for all sets. Olsson and Schubert (2007), on the other hand, propose that coherence be tied to the probability that the reporters are reliable rather than the truth of the reported propositions, a property Schubert and I refer to as *reliability conduciveness*. The setting is the same as the one used in my impossibility theorem in Olsson (2005), in which it is assumed that the quality of the reporters is unknown. They can be either perfectly reliable (truth-tellers) or completely unreliable, in the sense of generating their reports at random. This setting is often justified with reference to the quote from

---

[15] This is a very brief account of the impossibility theorem(s). A fuller discussion and explanation leading up to the statement and proof of my own theorem can be found in Olsson (2005), ch. 7. For a general discussion, see Olsson (2021b).

[16] A notable exception is Huemer (2011), who rejects the standard account of report independence.

C. I. Lewis regarding the independent reporters telling the same story (see Section 3.1). While Lewis is ultimately interested in the probability of what the reporters agree on, this probability, he thinks, is determined by the probability of truth-telling. Now a coherence measure is reliability conducive, as we define it, just in case a higher degree of coherence implies a higher probability that the reporters are reliable. As we demonstrate, my impossibility result regarding truth-conduciveness does not preclude coherence measures from being reliability conducive: even if more coherence fails to imply a higher probability of the reported propositions, more coherence may still imply a higher probability of truth-telling. This is perhaps not a great relief if we are only interested in the quality of the reporters because we wish to assess the truth of their reports. But, as Schubert (2011) points out, "we are sometimes [more] interested in the reliability of witnesses than in the truth of what they say" (p. 271):

> For instance, when testing students' abilities we are interested in the probability that they *know* the truth (i.e. that they are reliable) rather than in the probability that they *say* the truth (which they may do even though they do not know the truth). Also, in a trial, some questions to a witness may aim to show that the witness is unreliable (or reliable) rather than to show that what he or she says is the truth. Moreover, the legal theorists and philosophers within the Scandinavian School of Evidentiary Value argued that in a trial, we should be interested in the probability that there is a reliable connection between the evidence and the theme, rather than in the probability of the theme.[17]

Now as Schubert and I showed, while most established coherence measures, including the Glass–Olsson measure, fail to be reliability conducive, except in a trivial and uninteresting sense, even in a simple case with two equivalent reports, the Shogenji measure is, in fact, reliability conducive in such a setting. The Shogenji measure is also reliability conducive in scenarios with a finite number of equivalent reports (Schubert, 2012a) and in those with two overlapping, nonequivalent reports (Schubert, 2011). However, Schubert (2012b) proves two impossibility results, showing that no coherence measure is reliability conducive in all cases.

Angere (2007, 2008) retains the condition that all propositional sets are comparable but suggests weakening the tie between coherence and probability of a set of reported propositions to a mere statistical correlation. In other words, while no coherence measure is such that a higher degree of coherence, as measured, strictly implies a higher probability of the reported propositions,

---

[17] For an extended discussion of this connection to the Scandinavian School of Evidentiary Value, see Schubert and Olsson (2013).

there may be a strong statistical correlation between higher coherence and higher probability for some measures. To find out, Angere (2007) conducted extensive computer simulations involving, in his first study, sets of up to 12 reported propositions, comparing sets of the same size. He found that, for smaller sets, all measures considered were strongly correlated with high probability. However, as the sets grow larger, two measures perform significantly better than the others, namely, the Glass–Olsson measure and the Shogenji measure. Both exhibited a correlation of 83% for sets of reported propositions of size 12. Thus, for such sets, the more coherent set according to one of these measures was also jointly more probable in 83% of the cases.[18] In a second study in the same paper, Angere relaxed the ceteris paribus clause, allowing for comparison of sets of different size containing up to 15 propositions. In this test, the Glass–Olsson measure performed significantly better than the Shogenji measure when allowing for larger sets. For the former, the more coherent set was also jointly more probable in 87% of the cases, whereas the figure for the latter was a mere 72%. For the record, a measure proposed by Wouter Meijs (2006) was also included in Angere's studies. The Meijs measure performed much worse than the Glass–Olsson measure for larger sets in the first study, but in the second study the two measures performed roughly equally well, with the latter having a slight edge. I return to, and explain, the Meijs measure in Section 5.4.

Glass (2012) suggests that, rather than looking at the coherence of reported propositions, we should consider the coherence of the propositions with a hypothesis – and infer the hypothesis that coheres best with those propositions. Our example with Bert may serve to illustrate this main idea. The propositions under consideration, we recall, are Bert being at the crime scene (p), having a gun of the same type (q), and depositing a large sum of money (r). The traditional question has been whether the coherence of these reported propositions in some sense implies their joint truth. What Glass proposes is rather that we should look at various explanations of this set and ask which explanation is more coherent with the set. In this case, the explanation "Bert did it" seems highly coherent with p, q, and r and would be an obvious candidate for what Glass calls "inference to the most coherent explanation," abbreviated IMCE. Interestingly, Glass shows by computer simulation that if the Glass–Olsson measure is used, IMCE becomes very good at tracking the true hypothesis, and also very good at tracking the most probable hypothesis. This holds, in

---

[18] Dietrich and Moretti (2005) show that some coherence measures, notably the Glass–Olsson measure, guarantee that evidence that supports parts of a theory also supports the theory as a whole.

particular, if there is uncertainty concerning what prior probabilities we should assign the propositions involved.[19]

So far, the situation looks quite promising for the Glass–Olsson measure, despite it not being, in the strict sense, truth-conducive. After all, measuring coherence in the way it prescribes secures a high correlation with truth, both in Angere's and in Glass's sense. The Shogenji measure, too, is still an interesting measure from an epistemological perspective due to its reliability conduciveness in restricted, though important, cases and its convincing performance in Angere's investigations.[20]

However, as a coherence measure, the Glass–Olsson measure has a counter-intuitive feature, as Bovens and Hartmann (2003) were the first to note. To take their example, suppose we know that Tweety is a bird and that Tweety is a ground-dweller. The set of these two propositions is intuitively not very coherent: we would expect a bird not to be a ground-dweller and a ground-dweller not to be a bird. Now we learn that Tweety is a penguin. The new, extended set is intuitively more coherent than the original one. Yet Bovens and Hartmann showed that there are probability distributions under which the Glass–Olsson measure does not give this result, but rather the result that the sets are equally coherent (see Figure 2).

It gets still worse: Koscholke and Schippers (2016) prove that, on the Glass–Olsson measure, each subset of a given set of propositions is at least as coherent as the given set itself. In other words, we can never get a more coherent set by adding more propositions – the result will always be a set that is less or equally coherent. As a remedy, Koscholke and Schippers propose to measure coherence of a set in a way that is sensitive to the coherence of its subsets. On the revised measure, the coherence of a set equals the average Olsson–Glass coherence of its subsets (containing at least two propositions). The revised measure gives the intuitively correct result in Bovens and Hartmann's Tweety case. Koscholke, Schippers, and Stegman (2019) propose and defend another revision of the Glass–Olsson measure. It is unclear whether the revised Glass–Olsson measures perform as well as the original vis-à-vis the truth-related properties highlighted by Angere and Glass.

Bovens and Hartmann (2003) present a counterexample to the Shogenji measures as well. We are to assume that a crime has been committed and we are asked to compare two sets of reported propositions regarding their relative coherence. The set *S* contains the propositions "The culprit is either an African,

---

[19] I return to the assessment of prior probabilities in Section 5.5.

[20] Two obvious questions that seem to have gone unattended in the literature concern whether there are coherence measures that are (1) truth-conducive in restricted scenarios or (2) such that coherence is statistically correlated with higher reporter reliability.

Situation 1:

  $x_{1.1}$: Tweety is a bird.
  $x_{1.2}$: Tweety is a ground dweller.

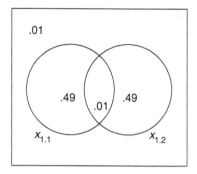

Situation 2:

  $x_{2.1}$: Tweety is a bird.
  $x_{2.2}$: Tweety is a ground dweller.
  $x_{2.3}$: Tweety is a penguin.

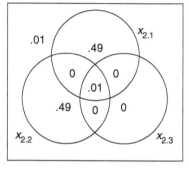

Figure 2 Situation 2 is intuitively more coherent than Situation 1, but the Glass–Olsson measure implies that they are equally coherent.

a North American, a South American, or a European" and "The culprit is not an Asian." The set S^* contains the propositions "The culprit is an African" and "The culprit is either Youssou (a particular African), Sulla (a particular South American), or Pierre (a particular European)". Since the propositions in S overlap completely whereas this is not the case for the propositions in S^* – indeed the latter show a low degree of overlap – S should be more coherent than S^*. However, Bovens and Hartmann show that there is a natural probability assignment to the propositions in S and S^* under which the Shogenji measure makes S^* more coherent than S.

Similarly, Siebel and Wolff (2008) argue that we have an intuition that equivalent reports are always maximally coherent, and that this is so independent of the prior probabilities of the reported propositions. As noted already in Olsson (2002c), however, the Shogenji coherence in such cases varies with the prior: the lower the prior, the higher the coherence. Siebel and Wolff provide the following example in support of their view (p. 170):

> Just imagine Detective Jones saying to his colleagues: 'If we have had no prior evidence for the robbers' being at least six feet tall, I would have said that Susan's and Tom's testimonies fit together very well. But it was already quite probable that the robbers are tall because another credible witness

assured us of this before we asked Susan and Tom. I must therefore admit that the latters' reports cohere only slightly.

Siebel and Wolff consider the last sentence to be counterintuitive, their conclusion being that coherence cannot be sensitive to the prior probability of the reported propositions. In Olsson (2002c), I noted that agreement on something less probable is more striking. I proposed, accordingly, that the Shogenji measure captures striking agreement. On this view, the upshot of Siebel and Wolff's argument is that striking agreement is not a form of coherence.[21][22]

What do we make of all this? Regarding the truth problem, it is difficult, if not impossible, to get around the theorem stating, essentially, that every coherence theory needs a weak foundation. The situation is different concerning the definition problem. The impossibility theorem states that no coherence measure is truth-conducive, but this property may be too strong and there are, as we saw, at least two promising alternative perspectives on what makes a coherence measure indicative of truth, and the Glass–Olsson measure does well on both accounts. Furthermore, we have the notion of reliability conduciveness and its connection to the Shogenji measure. Unfortunately, due to the counterexamples to both measures, neither seems defensible as a conceptual analysis of "degree of coherence."

Thus, it seems that, among the measures considered so far, the two best performers in relation to the most promising alternative accounts of the truth connection are, strictly speaking, not convincing coherence measures at all. If this is correct, there is little hope that even a coherence theory admitting a weak foundation can be resurrected in the light of alternative accounts of that connection. This is the somewhat perplexing situation in which we find ourselves.

In the remainder of this Element, I critically examine the recent debate about the proper definition of coherence from the perspective of Rudolf Carnap's methodology of explication (Carnap, 1950). In the process, I will direct serious criticism against common approaches to the explication of coherence in

---

[21] Schippers (2014b), similarly, argues that striking agreement is not a form of coherence. His analysis of striking agreement is similar to my account as presented here. The distinction between "agreement" and "striking agreement" was made already in Bovens and Olsson (2000).

[22] Coherence measures have been criticized for failing to handle inconsistent sets of propositions in the right way, and various test cases have been devised for this purpose (e.g. Schippers and Siebel, 2015). I have chosen not to discuss the application of coherence to inconsistent sets further in the present book. The setting here is the standard use of coherence for inferring the probability of joint truth of a set of propositions that typically represent belief contents. In the case of an inconsistent set, this is a trivial task in the sense that as soon as we know that the set is inconsistent, we also know that the propositions in the set are jointly false. While there may well be interesting uses of coherence as applied to inconsistent sets, such uses are not central in the present epistemological context.

probabilistic terms. The upshot will be a tentative and qualified defense of the Glass–Olsson measure.

4 Beyond Conceptual Analysis

4.1 Carnap's Method of Explication

The logical empiricist Rudolf Carnap introduced the method of explication in an attempt to introduce a more scientific approach to the definition of philosophical concepts.[23] While Carnap treats the topic in several publications, the locus classicus is the introductory chapter to Carnap (1950) where the method is presented in its mature form. By explication is there meant "the transformation of an inexact, prescientific concept, the explicandum, into a new exact concept, the explicatum" (p. 3). The purpose of an explication is to find a more precise concept that is to replace the explicandum in specialized contexts, analogous to the replacement of an ordinary knife with a scalpel in the operating room.

Since an explication maps an informal concept to a formal concept, the process of explication inherits a certain degree of vagueness and imprecision from the informal starting point. A consequence is that the process of explication is itself not an exact enterprise. In particular, there is no precise answer to the question whether a given explication is right or wrong. Rather, an explication should be assessed in relation to certain pragmatic considerations – which Carnap refers to as "desiderata" or "requirements" on an explicatum.

Explication is a two-step process, the first step involving what Carnap calls the "elucidation of the explicandum." This is the step at which it is made as clear as possible which informal concept is to be explicated. Carnap notes that this undertaking need not involve an outright definition of the explicandum but that it often suffices to give informal explanations and examples. The second step involves the search for a suitable formal correlate to the concept thus identified, something which in turn would first involve identifying the proper exact framework in which a suitable formal correlate can be found.

One of Carnap's examples concerns the term "true" as it occurs in natural language. A philosopher would naturally be more interested in some meanings than in others. Typically, the focus would be on the sense of "true" in "this sentence is true" rather than in "John is a true friend." Clarifying what informal meaning is intended would, in this case, be the first step in the explication process. Explicating the concept could, for instance, involve the specification of a theory of truth along the lines of Alfred Tarski and others in logical and set-theoretical terms.

---

[23] Sections 4.1 and 4.2 draw on the exposition of Carnap's methodology and explicationist epistemology in Olsson (2017a).

Let us suppose that the informal concept we are interested in has been identified with sufficient precision and, moreover, that we have an idea of what formal framework we wish to employ. What requirements should we place on a suitable explicatum in that framework? One requirement has already been mentioned, namely that of (increased) exactness. The whole purpose of explication is to define conceptual tools that allow for increased precision where it is needed. Yet, exactness is obviously not the only requirement on a suitable explicatum. While the exactness requirement precludes complete correspondence in meaning between a usually vague explicandum and a more exact explicatum, there obviously needs to be *some* such correspondence. Explicating "true" in such a way that the explicatum bears little or no resemblance to the ordinary meaning would be unacceptable in most philosophical inquiries, just as replacing a knife with a stethoscope in the operating room would.

The question is exactly how similar the explicatum needs to be to the explicandum. A natural suggestion is that the explicatum should be as similar to the explicandum as the latter's vagueness permits. This suggestion is, however, rejected by Carnap, who finds it to be undermined by scientific practice, which accepts scientific concepts that depart significantly from their counterparts in ordinary language if this departure is justified by increased precision but also increased fruitfulness. Carnap's own example involves the concept of fish, which previously included whales and seals but is, according to the *Encyclopedia Britannica*, now defined as "any of more than 30,000 species of cold-blooded vertebrate animals (phylum Chordata) found in the fresh and salt waters of the world."[24] The new definition is more fruitful in the sense that it can be used in the formulation of more empirical laws. Thus, unlike whales and seals, fish thus defined have a streamlined body for rapid swimming, extract oxygen from water using gills or use an accessory breathing organ to breathe atmospheric oxygen, have two sets of paired fins, lay eggs, and so on. The fish example is also interesting as a special case in which a scientific explication of an everyday concept was eventually adopted as the ordinary meaning of the term.

A more recent example is the 2006 redefinition of the concept planet by the International Astronomical Union (IAU), as described in Cordes and Siegwart (2019). A planet is now defined as "a celestial body that (a) is in orbit around the Sun, (b) has sufficient mass for its self-gravity to overcome rigid body forces so that it assumes a hydrostatic equilibrium (nearly round) shape, and (c) has

---

[24] "Fish," *Encyclopedia Britannica*, www.britannica.com/search?query=fish. Accessed March 27, 2022.

cleared the neighbourhood around its orbit" (IAU 2006). The new definition incorporates key aspects of the earlier use patterns, while at the same time being clearer and more fruitful (and simple). A notable consequence is that Pluto no longer qualifies as a planet.

Extrapolating from such examples of conceptual evolution in science and philosophy, Carnap states four requirements on a suitable explicatum (1950, p. 7):

1. The explicatum [the thing that explicates] is to be similar to the explicandum [the thing that is explicated] in such a way that, in most cases in which the explicandum has so far been used, the explicatum can be used; however, close similarity is not required, and considerable differences are permitted.
2. The characterization of the explicatum, that is, the rules of its use (for instance, in the form of a definition), is to be given in an exact form, so as to introduce the explicatum into a well-connected system of scientific concepts.
3. The explicatum is to be a fruitful concept, that is, useful for the formulation of many universal statements (empirical laws in the case of a nonlogical concept, logical theorems in the case of a logical concept).
4. The explicatum should be as simple as possible; this means as simple as the more important requirements 1, 2, and 3 permit.

The fourth requirement – of simplicity – is the least important and is essentially only invoked as a tiebreaker, Carnap submits; if several potential explicata of a given explicandum are equal regarding requirements 1–3 but show a marked difference in simplicity, "the scientist will, as a rule, prefer the simplest of them" (p. 7). As he also explains, "[t]he simplicity of a concept may be measured, in the first place, by the simplicity of the form of its definition and, second, by the simplicity of the forms of the laws connecting it with other concepts" (ibid.).

Carnap's exhaustive division of scientific concepts into two kinds – empirical and logical – was a cornerstone of the logical empiricist movement of which he was a leading figure, though from a contemporary perspective it makes his account of fruitfulness seem unnecessarily restrictive. Little prevents us from allowing other kinds of concept to appear as explicanda, for instance legal or ethical concepts, in an updated version of Carnap's account. Moreover, it seems that any improvement of a theory occasioned by the addition of a concept would count in favor of the fruitfulness of the latter, and not only improvement occasioned by the addition of new laws or theorems. Thus, we may distinguish between narrow ("nomological," "theorem-oriented") and broad ("holistic") fruitfulness and, correspondingly, between a narrow and a broad approach to explication. These concerns, however, though generally important, are of no consequence to my application of Carnap's method in this Element.

Carnap, usefully for our purposes as it turns out, distinguishes three different kinds of concept: classificatory, comparative, and quantitative. Classificatory concepts serve to classify things into two kinds. The concept *warm* would be one example. A comparative concept relates one thing to another, as when we say that one thing is warmer than another. A quantitative concept such as temperature, by contrast, serves to describe something with a numerical value, whereby the values "are found either directly through measurement or indirectly by calculation from other values of the same or other concepts" (p. 9). Comparative concepts stand between the two other kinds and can be used when it is not possible to quantify the property in question.

Classificatory concepts are the simplest and least efficient kind, Carnap thinks. Comparative concepts are more powerful and quantitative concepts still more, in the sense that they enable us to give a more precise description of a situation and, more importantly, to formulate more comprehensive general laws. Therefore, the historical development of concepts, he observes, often follows the path from a classificatory concept to a comparative concept, culminating in a quantitative concept, such as temperature, which requires a more elaborate scientific framework of measurement.

Carnap thinks that quantitative concepts can be seen as explications of their comparative counterparts. Thus, temperature can be seen as an explication of something being warmer than something else, where the latter is viewed as a concept defined with reference to the sensation of heat. In this particular case, the process of explication eventually led to a change in the meaning of "warmer," which is now used in the sense of "having a higher temperature." In this respect, temperature is similar to the revised concept of fish, which, as I noted, is roughly the one now used in everyday life. Now temperature has, of course, proved its great fruitfulness by the fact that it occurs in many important laws. Such attempts to employ quantitative concepts in the formulation of laws are not always successful, Carnap notes, even if they are well defined by exact rules of measurement (p. 14). Carnap mentions attempts to define quantitative concepts in psychology as cases in point.

4.2 Explicationist Epistemology

Following the terminology introduced in Olsson (2017a), I will use "explicationist philosophy" to refer to the application of Carnap's method to philosophy and "explicationist epistemology" to its application in the theory of knowledge.[25] Carnap's choice to refer to similarity, fruitfulness, exactness, and simplicity as "requirements" strongly suggests that all four should be given positive weight in the explication process. This is what gives explicationist philosophy its unique flavor in relation to other methodologies, which can be seen as limiting cases of explication, in the sense that some requirements are disregarded. For instance, mid-twentieth-century Oxford-style ordinary language philosophy results from a sole focus on maximizing similarity between the explicandum and the explicatum. Alternatively – and more interestingly in the present context – other methodologies can be regarded as sub-methodologies for elucidating the explicandum or assessing the extent to which Carnap's requirements are satisfied for a given proposed explicatum (Olsson, 2017a). From this perspective, ordinary language philosophy can be useful for identifying the ordinary concept to be explicated, but also in assessing the degree to which the similarity requirement is satisfied in a given case. The same is true of experimental philosophy in the tradition of Stephen Stich and others (e.g., Weinberg, Nichols, and Stich, 2001). Where the ordinary language school tried to determine ordinary use through the armchair reasoning of a presumed expert user (the philosopher him- or herself), the experimentalist's method of choice is to conduct psychological experiments involving laymen subjects.

As Carnap noted, it is often sufficiently clear what possible meanings a given term has, in which case there is agreement on the possible explicanda. In cases where it cannot be taken for granted what the possible explicanda are, the obvious solution is to seek guidance in the relevant empirical science, which is lexicology, the study of word meanings. Thus, we need to consult an authoritative dictionary. In the case of the philosophically contested term "knowledge," for instance, Lexico (formerly Oxford Living Dictionaries) lists several pre-systematic meanings.[26] "Knowledge" can refer to "[f]acts, information, and skills acquired through experience or education; the theoretical or

---

[25] I treat the Gettier problem from the perspective of explicationist epistemology in Olsson (2015), arguing that the problem is not a knockdown argument against any account of knowledge if that account is viewed as an explication rather than as a conceptual analysis. The reason is that Gettier examples are too rare to disqualify by themselves a proposed explicatum from being sufficiently similar to the explicandum. I am not aware of any book-length study in epistemology making both explicit and systematic use of the method of explication. Carnap's own study of confirmation measures (Carnap, 1950) is thematically closer to philosophy of science. Keith Lehrer (1990) explicitly commits to the method but arguably does not make systematic use of it, settling in the end for a highly complex explication of knowledge. In his book on the contextualist approach to knowledge, Peter Baumann (2016) commits to Carnap's method but employs it only sporadically. As I argue in Olsson (2017a), Goldman (1999), in justifying his choice to view knowledge as simply true belief for the purposes of social epistemology, makes systematic use of a similar method, although he does not attribute its reconstructivist character to Carnap.

[26] "Knowledge," Lexico, www.lexico.com/definition/knowledge. Accessed January 6, 2022.

practical understanding of a subject." It can also denote "the sum of what is known," as in the expression "the transmission of knowledge." A further sense is knowledge as "information held on a computer system." The dictionary also lists, under the same mass term heading, a particular use explicitly noted as belonging to philosophy: "[t]rue, justified belief; certain understanding, as opposed to opinion." One cited example is: "As a rationalist, he believed that the only path to true knowledge was through logic." According to the same source, knowledge can signify "[a]wareness or familiarity gained by experience of a fact or situation." At least some of the confusion in epistemology can be attributed to a difference in the starting point of the epistemological project (cf. Olsson, 2017a). An initial focus on "knowledge" in the sense of "the theoretical or practical understanding of a subject" naturally suggests an internalist approach in which the subject's access to her own knowledge and the relations between her beliefs are central, whereas if the point of departure is "knowledge" in the sense of "[a]wareness or familiarity gained by experience of a fact or situation," the likely outcome is an externalist theory that emphasizes the relation between the subject and the world.

There is usually not only a plurality of explicanda, but also a plurality of explicata for a given explicandum. This is a consequence of the fact that the goodness of an explicatum is a matter of satisfying all the four Carnapian requirements – similarity, fruitfulness, exactness, and simplicity – to a sufficient degree as a package, together with the observation that there are inherent tensions between these requirements. As for the latter, there is a potential conflict between similarity, on the one hand, and fruitfulness and exactness, on the other, as Carnap's fish example illustrates. Our ordinary concepts have developed because they are useful tools relative to the concerns of ordinary life. It is hardly surprising that they often turn out to be less useful when the context shifts to highly specialized activities, such as scientific inquiry. In such cases, science often opts for the more fruitful and exact understanding of a term at the expense of close agreement with ordinary use. Also, a more complex explicatum may be more fruitful than a simple one. What explicatum is chosen as the explication of a given explicandum will in the end depend on the context, but also, more fundamentally, on the theoretical prefer-ences of the explicationist, such as the extent to which she is willing to depart from ordinary use in the interest of harvesting other theoretical goods.

To illustrate the plurality of explicata for a given explicandum, consider again the meaning of knowledge as justified, true belief (JTB). Admittedly, this is noted in the preceding dictionary as an already specialized, philosophical meaning, but the fact that it is listed at all indicates that it, to some extent, has made its entrance also in ordinary language and thought. At any rate, anyone familiar with contemporary epistemology will know that there is a multitude of attempts to give a more precise account of knowledge, using the JTB meaning as the starting point. Most of the disagreement centers around the concept of justification, of which there are various accounts that purport to be more exact or at least more enlightening. Not all such accounts would qualify as Carnapian explications because they fail to live up to one or more of the four requirements, ironically often that of exactness, a difficulty for which internalist accounts of justification seem particularly amenable.[27] An externalist account, by contrast, can achieve a considerable degree of exactness by invoking the scientifically respectable, though by no means philosophically unproblematic, concept of a reliable process of belief formation (cf. Olsson, 2015). The JTB meaning of knowledge does not specify the degree of justification required for knowing. This problem is solved in the specialized context of criminal law by stipulating that a conclusion is justified and legally known, in the sense that legal inquiry needs to proceed no further, if it has been established "beyond reasonable doubt." Risto Hilpinen's (1991) account of the argumentative conception of knowledge is another plausible example of an explication of the JTB sense of knowledge, in his case in a context in which it is useful to view belief systems more generally as information systems. Hilpinen's theory achieves semiformal clarity regarding several traditional questions that arise for the JTB account (cf. Olsson, 2022).

As I have already hinted, there is a third sense in which explicationist epistemology is pluralistic, namely in that of allowing for a plurality of sub-methodologies. The various methodological schools that exist in epistemology and philosophy generally need not be seen as competing paradigms but can be

---

[27] A complicating factor is that the term justification is, according to the Cambridge Dictionary, itself ambiguous between "a good reason or explanation of something." This means that a further elucidation of "justified" is needed before the project of identifying a suitable explicatum can take off. See Lycan (2002) for the effect of focusing, on my reconstruction, on the less common explanatory meaning of justification in epistemology. Alston, in his influential 1993 paper, makes a similar point when he infers the diversity of the pre-systematic meanings of "justification" from epistemologists' very different accounts of the concept (p. 534): "If we take the full range of parties to the disputes we have been considering, some of whom have had their thinking about 'epistemic justification' nourished primarily by some of the roots just mentioned and others about others, there does not seem to be enough commonality in their pre-theoretical understanding of the nature of epistemic justification to warrant us in supposing that there is some uniquely identifiable item about which they hold different views. It seems, rather, that they are highlighting, emphasizing, 'pushing' different concepts, all called 'justification'. It seems, to switch to the perspective of this paper, that they are selecting different epistemic desiderata, or packages thereof, as deserving of the honorific title 'justification'." Thus, what Alston calls epistemic desiderata in relation to justification are, in Carnap's terminology, the different explicanda of the term. However, Alston's focus is on understanding the nature and interrelations of the explicanda and not to replace them by other more precise concepts for specialized purposes. See Olsson (2017a) for a more extensive comparison between Alston's and Carnap's methodologies.

viewed, rather, as complementary methods under an explicationist methodo-logical umbrella. For example, a dictionary will only take you so far in eluci-dating the ordinary meaning of central epistemological terms that could be usefully explicated. Ordinary language philosophy, philosophical intuition-probing, and experimental studies may be necessary for making more delicate distinctions in the meaning of words. These methods are also potentially useful in the assessment of the similarity of a proposed explicatum with the chosen explicandum. Furthermore, formal epistemology, the study of knowledge by logical or mathematical means, has so far resulted in an impressive catalog of potentially more exact explicata of knowledge and other epistemological con-cepts (see, for instance, Hendricks, 2006). Having such a catalog at our disposal is likely to be useful when the need arises for increased precision and higher scientific and philosophical standards in our epistemological investigations.

5 Explicating Coherence

5.1 Early Accounts of Coherence as Explications

It is time to revisit the early accounts of coherence and consider them not as conceptual analyses but as explications of coherence. The first question we need to ask is to what extent they are explications of coherence at all, that is, to what extent they are more precise versions of one of the presystematic meanings of "coherence." To determine these meanings, we should, as I have argued, consult authoritative lexica rather than rely on our own linguistic intuitions.

In the case of "coherence," unlike "knowledge," there is agreement in accessible dictionaries on only a few basic meanings. The *Merriam-Webster* dictionary defines coherence, in the first instance, as "the quality or state of cohering." A quality or state can cohere in virtue of "systematic or logical connection or consistency," as in "The essay as a whole lacks coherence." It can also, we are told, cohere in virtue of the "integration of diverse elements, relationships, or values," as in "The various parts of this house – discrete in color, in shape, in placement – join together with remarkable coherence." Second, "coherence" can also refer to "the property of being coherent," as in "a plan that lacks coherence." *Merriam-Webster* lists the following synonyms: "balance," "concinnity," "consonance," "consonancy," "harmony," "orchestra-tion," "proportion," "symmetry," "symphony," and "unity."[28] Similar defin-itions are found in other lexica. For example, the *Cambridge Dictionary* defines coherence as "the situation when the parts of something fit together in a natural or reasonable way," as in "There was no coherence between the first

---

[28] "Coherence," *Merriam-Webster.com Dictionary*, www.merriam-webster.com/dictionary/coher-ence. Accessed January 6, 2022.

and the second halves of the movie."[29] Finally, *Lexico* lists two meanings: "the quality of being logical and consistent," as in "This raises further questions on the coherence of state policy," and "the quality of forming a unified whole," as in "the group began to lose coherence and the artists took separate directions."[30]

The specific kind of *epistemic* coherence that is relevant in epistemology is a specialized kind that is not separately defined in standard lexica. However, it is close to the first meaning mentioned in *Merriam-Webster* – "systematic or logical connection or consistency." It can also be seen as a special case of the "integration of diverse elements, relationships, or values," namely, insofar as those elements, relationships, or values are of an epistemic kind and concern beliefs, inference relations between beliefs, and so on. In the following, as before, "coherence" abbreviates "epistemic coherence."

Ewing's and Lewis's definitions are obviously closely related to the preceding lexicon definitions. Ewing, as we saw, defined a coherent set as one that is logically consistent and such that each proposition follows logically from the other propositions taken together. This proposal is very close to the first meaning of coherence noted in *Merriam-Webster*, namely coherence in virtue of "systematic or logical connection or consistency." Since Ewing's proposal is more exact than this explicandum in spelling out that "logical" should have its narrow sense of formal (classical) logic and how the propositions should be thus related, it is certainly a candidate explicatum for that explicandum. I noted before, however, that sets that seem intuitively coherent often fail to satisfy Ewing's definition, which I therefore deemed too narrow as a conceptual analysis. However, given Carnap's liberal view on the similarity between the explicandum and explicatum, this is at least not a knockdown argument now that we are considering, instead, Ewing's proposal as an explication; we recall that, on Carnap's view, "close similarity is not required, and considerable differences are permitted." So far, so good. However, Carnap also mentioned a minimum level of similarity, which is satisfied when "in most cases in which the explicandum has so far been used, the explicatum can be used." In Ewing's case, it is at best unclear whether even this minimal requirement is satisfied. Lewis's definition in terms of probabilistic rather than (narrowly) logical support between propositions is more promising in this regard, although in his case, too, the extent to which it satisfies Carnap's minimal requirement on similarity will ultimately have to be decided by empirical means. If we assume, for the sake of the argument, that it does, we can also observe that it has the advantage of being both exact and strikingly simple. The question remains how

---

[29] "Coherence," *Cambridge Dictionary*, https://dictionary.cambridge.org/dictionary/english/coherence. Accessed January 6, 2022.

[30] "Coherence," Lexico, www.lexico.com/definition/coherence. Accessed January 6, 2022.

it fares regarding fruitfulness. For an orthodox Carnapian, a fruitful concept, we recall, is one that can be plugged into empirical laws (in the case of an empirical concepts) or logical theorems (in the case of a logical concept). Unfortunately, Lewis's theory of coherence does not shed much light on the fruitfulness of his account in either of these senses. He does not suggest how coherence in his sense is an empirically relevant concept; nor does he prove any theorems in probability theory featuring his concept of coherence. I am not aware of any other empirical, logical, or mathematical investigations in which Lewis's concept plays a prominent role. Finally, both Ewing and Lewis define coherence as a matter of all-or-nothing, that is, coherence comes out as what Carnap called a mere classificatory concept. As we saw, Carnap thought that classificatory concepts are the simplest and least efficient kind.

Let us, similarly, consider BonJour's criteria from the explicationist perspective. I repeat them here for ease of reference:

1. A system of beliefs is coherent only if it is logically consistent.
2. A system of beliefs is coherent in proportion to its degree of probabilistic consistency.
3. The coherence of a system of beliefs is increased by the presence of inferential connections between its component beliefs and increased in proportion to the number and strength of such connections.
4. The coherence of a system of beliefs is diminished to the extent to which it is divided into subsystems of beliefs that are relatively unconnected to each other by inferential connections.
5. The coherence of a system of beliefs is decreased in proportion to the presence of unexplained anomalies in the believed content of the system.

Comparing these criteria to the explicanda we identified in standard dictionaries, we see that criteria 1 and 2 are variations on the theme that coherence requires consistency. This is evident regarding criterion 1, which requires of a coherent set that it be logically consistent. Criterion 2 is intuitively a stronger requirement of consistency: even if a system is logically consistent, some belief may be improbable given the other beliefs, in which case criterion 1 would be satisfied but criterion 2 violated. Moreover, criteria 3 and 4 capture the equally common notion that coherence results from "systematic or logical connection" between the parts of a system. Criterion 5, concerning anomalies, is more difficult to motivate in terms of consistency or logical connectivity. One way of justifying this criterion is by connecting it with the idea of a coherent system as a "unified whole," which we found in *Lexico* and, albeit less clearly expressed, in *Merriam-Webster*, the proposal being that a system that contains explanatory gaps fails to qualify as a unified whole. From this perspective, a system is a unified whole if it is explanatorily complete: every belief in the system can be explained by other beliefs in that system.

Whereas criteria 1 to 4 can be seen as attempts to clarify the first sense of coherence mentioned in *Merriam-Webster*, that involving "systematic or logical connection or consistency," both *Merriam-Webster* and *Lexico* list the "unified whole" sense of coherence, to which 5 could be tied, as a separate meaning. This observation calls into question the idea that the package of coherence criteria (1–5) elucidate or explicate one single explicandum. A further difficulty when viewing BonJour's account from an explicationist perspective is that his criteria make use of two kinds of concept. In 1, coherence is seen as an all-or-nothing classificatory concept. The reference to increase and decrease in coherence in the other criteria suggests, by contrast, a quantitative notion. On closer examination, however, the criteria fail to deliver even a comparative account of coherence because, for reasons already mentioned, they fail to indicate, for every pair of systems, which one is more coherent than the other. Already for this reason, the criteria, besides falling short with regard to exactness, hardly satisfy the fruitfulness requirement either.

To what extent Thagard's theory of explanatory coherence qualifies as an explication is a complex question, to which I cannot do justice here. I will rest content with making a few remarks on the matter. We saw that Thagard's theory consists in a number of principles relating coherence to other concepts such as, most importantly, explanation. As such, his theory consists of a number of axioms or postulates, and is, strictly speaking, not a definition. However, judged by the exact phrasing of Carnap's exactness requirement, this fact does not by itself rule out Thagard's account being an explication. We recall that the characterization of the explicatum is to be given in an exact form "*for instance, in the form of a definition*" (my emphasis). Having said that, Carnap argues against the Peano axioms for the natural numbers being an explication of the concept of a natural number because the axioms admit different concrete interpretations. Presumably, he would have raised similar concerns regarding Thagard's principles, which could be satisfied in quite different formal frameworks. It is, therefore, more plausible to view a particular interpretation of Thagard's principles in a given formal framework (such as neutral networks), rather than the principles themselves, as an explication.

5.2 The Shogenji Measure as an Explication of Coherence

As I have argued, the perhaps most prominent early attempts to define coherence are not very promising as explications of that concept. This is not necessarily the case for the more recent coherence measures that have been proposed in the literature, which have the advantage of being exactly defined quantitative concepts. Stefan Schubert (at the time a PhD student of mine) was probably the first to suggest that coherence measures be evaluated, not as conceptual analyses, but as explications in Carnap's sense (Schubert 2011 and 2012a). Indeed, Schubert gives a systematic argument in favor of the suitability of the Shogenji measure from this perspective, referring to all four Carnapian requirements.

The justification of the Shogenji measure as an explication of coherence is preceded, in Schubert (2012a), by a discussion of the aforementioned counterexamples to that measure (p. 315). In response to the Bovens and Hartmann example, Schubert distinguishes what he calls "two concepts of coherence," namely, agreement and striking agreement. We recall that the set S contains the propositions "The culprit is either an African, a North American, a South American, or a European" and "The culprit is not an Asian," whereas the set S^* contains the propositions "The culprit is an African" and "The culprit is either Youssou (a particular African), Sulla (a particular South American), or Pierre (a particular European)." Bovens and Hartmann showed that there are probability assignments such that, counterintuitively, S^* is more coherent than S on the Shogenji measure. Schubert remarks that "S no doubt shows a greater degree of agreement than S^*" (p. 315), but, he adds, "intuitions are not as clear when it comes to striking agreement" (ibid.). Since, on Bovens and Hartmann's probability assignment, the propositions in S^* have much lower prior probabilities, the fact that they "agree to quite a large extent may be considered rather surprising" (ibid.). Hence, Schubert concludes, "it is conceivable that intuitions that tell against the Shogenji measure derive from the agreement concept whereas the Shogenji measure rather aims to capture the concept of striking agreement" (ibid.).

Schubert notes, however, that there is also the Siebel and Wolff counterexample to consider. The example, we recall, was intended to show that the coherence of a set of propositions cannot depend on the prior probabilities of those propositions. Since the Shogenji measure makes coherence dependent on these priors, it fails to be an adequate coherence measure, or so Siebel and Wolff conclude. In response, Schubert gives an example intended to support the opposite intuition. In the example, we are asked to compare two sets of full agreement. In the first case, the witnesses agree on "The murderer was a very tall man. He was limping and seemed to have trouble breathing" (P). Call the set of these two reports S. In the second case, the witnesses agree on "The murderer was a man" (Q). Call this set S'. Schubert remarks (2012a), p. 316:

> Since P is a much more specific proposition than Q, S is intuitively more
> coherent than S'. And, since P under normal circumstances has a much lower

prior probability than Q, there is a negative correlation between the prior probability of what the witnesses agree upon and the degree of coherence in this case. That is just the way striking agreement, and, in particular, the Shogenji measure, would have it.

Following this discussion, Schubert proceeds to assume, for the sake of the argument, that the Shogenji measure is to some extent at odds with our pre-systematic concept of coherence, asking whether that would show that it is not a plausible *explication* of that concept. He argues that it does not show this, noting that similarity to the pretheoretical concept, the explicandum, is only one of Carnap's four requirements; there are also the requirements of exactness, fruitfulness, and simplicity, and, he adds, "the Shogenji measure is a very plausible explication of coherence according to the other criteria" (Schubert, 2011), p. 316:

> Firstly, it is couched in probabilistic terms, making it very exact. Secondly, the fact that the Shogenji measure is the only measure with an independent standing in the literature that is reliability conducive arguably makes it very fruitful for the epistemologist. For, as we have seen, several informal coherence theorists have conjectured that coherence is connected to reliability; a conjecture that the Shogenji measure manages to explicate. Thirdly, it is also a simple explication; for example, it is notably simpler than Douven and Meijs's measures. Thus we see that the Shogenji measure fulfills the criteria 2–4 very well.

A similar argument leads to the following conclusion in Schubert (2011), p. 271:

> Thus we see that the Shogenji measure and ordinally equivalent measures perform very well on the criteria (2)–(4), something which makes any argument which focuses only on similarity to the pre-theoretical concept (criterion 1) seriously incomplete. As for criterion 1, we have seen that there are reasons to believe that the Shogenji measure does mirror one pre-systematic notion of coherence, namely striking agreement. Hence the Shogenji measure (and ordinally equivalent measures) is an epistemologically fruitful explication of coherence which have a claim to being in close correspondence with one of our pre-theoretical conceptions of that notion.[31]

Hence, Schubert thinks that agreement and striking agreement are two concepts of coherence, that the Shogenji measure mirrors one of these concepts, namely striking agreement, and, finally, that coherence thus explicated is an epistemically fruitful concept.

---

[31] Ordinal equivalence refers to the property measures have when they induce the same order of the sets to which they are applied.

However, given the counterexamples to the Shogenji measure and in particular the Siebel–Wolff example, Schubert's case for thinking that it mirrors one use of the term coherence still seems rather weak. Moreover, no easily accessible standard lexicon lists "striking agreement" or a synonymous term among the meanings of "coherence." For instance, *Lexico* lists two meanings of "coherence": "the quality of being logical and consistent" and "the quality of forming a unified whole," neither of which seems in any obvious way related to "striking agreement." Nor is coherence a form of striking agreement, for that matter. The term "striking agreement" does not occur at all in standard lexica. The closest term that does is presumably "coincidence," which, according to *Merriam and Webster*, has essentially one meaning, namely, "the occurrence of events that happen at the same time by accident but seem to have some connection." In the epistemological case, coincidence would refer to the occurrence of reports that happen by accidence but seem to have some connection. There is no reference to coherence or its synonyms here.

This does not mean that the Shogenji measure does not capture "striking agreement" (or "report coincidence") but only that the latter, as Siebel and Wolff concluded, *is not a form of coherence*. Nor does it mean that striking agreement is not an epistemologically interesting concept in its own right; Schubert's work on reliability conduciveness, with or without my coauthorship, arguably shows that it is, even if, as Schubert finally managed to establish, no measure is reliability conducive in general. For these reasons, a more plausible upshot of Schubert's innovative justification of the Shogenji measure is that the latter is an epistemologically fruitful explication, not of coherence, but of striking agreement.

5.3 The Glass–Olsson Measure as an Explication of Coherence

Schubert (2011) remarks, after his attempted justification of the Shogenji measures as an explication of coherence (p. 271):

> This is not to say that it is the only legitimate explication of coherence. Angere (2008) suggests that even though coherence does not imply truth in general, a greater degree of coherence can still be seen as an indication of truth, and hence it is still useful as a rule-of-thumb. The most useful coherence measure, i.e., the one that is the best indicator of truth, is, according to Angere's test, the Olsson measure (Olsson, 2002[c]) ... which was found to be reliability conducive only in a trivial sense in (Olsson and Schubert 2007).

In line with my earlier work (starting with Olsson, 2002c), Schubert thinks of the Glass–Olsson measures as a measure of coherence. However, as we saw, this measure has the consequence that we cannot gain coherence by adding more reported propositions and yet, intuitively, we do gain coherence by adding "Tweety is a penguin" to the set consisting of "Tweety is a bird" and "Tweety is a ground-dweller." The former is the "missing piece" that, when added, turns the latter set into a unified whole. Hence, I now think that it is problematic to think of the Glass–Olsson measure as capturing coherence.

The conclusion that the Glass–Olsson is not a measure of coherence is compatible with my proposal in Olsson (2002c) that it is a measure of agreement. The problem was that I there assumed – wrongly, I now think – that agreement is a form of coherence. In fact, a natural conclusion of the Tweety examples is precisely that the Glass–Olsson measure captures agreement but not coherence. For a measure of agreement, we would expect that we do not get more of it by adding more reported propositions; by adding more propositions, we can only retain or lose agreement, never increase it. In the Tweety case, adding "Tweety is a penguin" increases coherence, but, arguably, it does not increase agreement. The latter is exactly what the Glass–Olsson measure implies. The claim that agreement is not a form of coherence is also supported by standard lexica, which – as we have seen – do not list agreement as one of the meanings of "coherence."[32] Nor, for that matter, do they list "coherence" or its synonyms as a meaning of "agreement."

It might be objected that there is also partial agreement, however, which may raise total agreement. For example, "Tweety is a penguin" can be taken to partly agree with "Tweety is a bird" and "Tweety is a ground-dweller" because the former is analytically implied by it and the latter is a biological consequence. Hence, if "Tweety is a penguin" is added to the other propositions, there are more relations of agreement, resulting in a higher total agreement, so the argument goes (thanks to a reviewer for raising this point). However, the last claim, that more relations of agreement result in higher total agreement, strikes me as not generally true. Take a case of five witnesses giving exactly the same testimony – "Smith was at the crime scene," say. Now comes the sixth witness giving a partially but not fully agreeing testimony – "Smith or Jones was at the crime scene," say. There is a sense in which there are now "more relations of agreement," but the overall agreement is nevertheless lower. After all, before the sixth witness came along, the witnesses were in full agreement, which is not the case thereafter.

Again, I essentially agree with Schubert's reasoning, except, to repeat, that I view the Glass–Olsson measure as an epistemologically useful explication, not

---

[32] This is so even though the lexica in question mention properties, such as logical connection, consistency, and fitting together, that are implied by agreement: if propositions are in full agreement, they are logically connected (by deductive entailment) in addition to being (typically) consistent and fitting together.

of coherence, but of agreement. In the justification of that conclusion, I would furthermore point not only to Angere's work, but also to Glass's study of inference to the most coherent explanation, a context in which the Glass–Olsson measure, once more, does particularly well. Both Angere's and Glass's work support, in Carnap's sense, the epistemological fruitfulness of the latter measure. For the sake of completeness, one should add, of course, that the Glass–Olsson measure is not only exact but also very simple, an advantage it shares with the Shogenji measure.

My conclusion that the Glass–Olsson, while measuring agreement, is not a measure of coherence is compatible with the constraint on coherence measures proposed by Siebel and Wolff (2008) to the effect that any set of equivalent (fully agreeing) reports is maximally coherent. This is, as I observed, the constraint at work in their counterexample to the Shogenji measure. As Siebel and Wolff note, the Glass–Olsson measure satisfies this constraint. However, this does not make it a coherence measure. The constraint is not a sufficient condition on measures of coherence, something that does not prevent it from being a necessary condition.

5.4 Koscholke and Schippers on Coherence Measures as Explications

So far, my conclusion in this section is that, while two measures that have been presented as coherence measures are epistemologically useful explications, they are not explications *of coherence* but of other, related explicanda. We have not encountered a measure that is an epistemologically useful explication of the central notion of coherentism, namely, coherence itself. This is hardly an ideal situation from a coherentist perspective. It looks very much like a further disappointment for the coherentist, in addition to the discouragement caused by the negative solution to the truth problem and the impossibility results.

A recurring problem in the preceding discussion was that the supposed explications of coherence were found to be insufficiently similar to the explicandum. A natural question to ask is therefore whether any of the other proposed measures of coherence in the literature are more convincing in this regard. If such measures can be found, the next question to ask would be to what extent they satisfy the other requirements as well, in particular, fruitfulness and simplicity (exactness is already secured by their probabilistic formulations). But first things first.

Arguably, some of the most advanced and creative studies of the similarity of coherence measures to the intended explicandum are due to two German scholars in the younger generation: Jakob Koscholke and Michael Schippers.

Both make explicit use of Carnap's method of explication. For this purpose, they have employed three procedures. One consists in assessing the performance of coherence measures against normative judgments about paradigmatic test cases in which we, supposedly, have a clear intuition about one set being more coherent than another (Koscholke, 2016). Another involves assessing the measures against proposed adequacy constraints (Schippers, 2014a). These procedures share the potential limitation that they rely on particular philosophers' judgments about test cases and adequacy constraints, respectively. The third method involves, instead, comparing the verdict of the measures in test cases with recruited layman subjects' assessments in an experimental setting (Koscholke and Jekel, 2017), the main question being how good the measures are at predicting the subjects' assessments of relative coherence.

Koscholke (2016), pp. 155–156, explicitly relates his study to Carnap's method of explication:

> Probabilistic coherence measures are functions assigning real numbers to sets of propositions under some joint probability distribution. At best, the assigned numbers represent how good the respective propositions fit or hang together, agree with or mutually support each other – briefly, how coherent the propositions are. At worst, they do not. Hence, the development of probabilistic measures of coherence . . . can be understood as a search for a quantitative explication – in the sense of Carnap (1950) – of the concept of coherence.

Koscholke proceeds to discuss the requirement of similarity:

> Of course, in order to be an explication at all, the explicandum – here, the concept of coherence – and the explicatum – here, a probabilistic coherence measure – have to be similar (besides the explicatum having to be exact, fruitful and simple). To ensure this kind of similarity several authors . . . have formulated adequacy constraints for probabilistic coherence measures . . . Adequacy constraints can therefore be considered as serving as reference points for the evaluation of a coherence measure's adequacy.

The relevance of test cases is explained as follows:

> Test cases for probabilistic coherence measures are paradigmatic situations providing information about a specified set of propositions such that the values of a probabilistic coherence measure for this set can be computed. Most important, test cases come with a normative coherence assessment for the respective set based on considerations regarding the situation in which the set is located. The evaluation is then quite simple. If some measure's values in a certain test case are in accordance with the normative coherence assessment provided by this case and the assessment has strong intuitive support, then the measure remains a candidate for an adequate measure of coherence.

If a measure's value is not in accordance with the assessment, its credibility as an adequate coherence measure decreases.

Before studying how well various proposed coherence measures do in relation to the test cases, Koscholke (2016), p. 161, cautions:

It is, however, worth noticing that the variety of motivations underlying the different proposals shows that the proponents aimed at explicating different aspects of the concept of coherence. This indicates that there might be more than a single probabilistic coherence measure ... suggesting that we should be pluralists with respect to the concept of coherence and probabilistic measures of coherence.

Exactly what is meant by pluralism here is not quite clear, however. Claiming that proponents of various measures aimed at explicating "different aspects of the concept of coherence" can mean either that they were interested in different intuitive meanings of coherence, that is, different explicanda, or that they were interested in one and the same intuitive meaning of coherence but that this meaning could be captured using different formal accounts, that is, different explicata.

The proposed coherence measures studied by Koscholke (2016) are listed in Appendix A. The test cases can be found in Appendix B. As a preliminary, I will raise some methodological concerns. I then comment, in general terms, on the test results and proceed to the results for the Glass–Olsson and Shogenji measures, in particular. A discussion of the performance of more complex measures concludes this section.

Although Koscholke's (2016) systematic study of coherence measures in relation to test cases is extremely useful, there are some methodological issues that need to be raised. First, while the article discusses many (11) test cases, they do not exhaust the list of examples in the literature. For instance, both the African culprit example in Bovens and Hartmann (2003) and the detective example in Siebel and Wolff (2008) are missing – we encountered both in Section 3.3. In Carnapian terms, the investigation can at best establish that some measures are more similar to the explicandum than others from the perspective of the test cases employed; not that they are more similar to the explicandum simpliciter. Second, some of the test cases originate from authors who also proposed coherence measures that are included in the same test (Douven, Glass, Meijs, and Schupbach). An even more convincing test would include only test cases that have an independent standing in relation to what is being tested, although it may be argued that this condition is already satisfied if the intuitive reaction to the test cases is clear and uniform. Third, all the tests, except the Tweety case, involve only comparisons between sets of the same size. This, too, is a limitation to be considered when interpreting the results, as is, finally, the fact that all sets are small.[33] These remarks also affect the spin-off study in Koscholke and Jekel (2017) and other works referring to these studies for support (e.g., Schippers, 2014a, 2014b).

Turning now to the results, some test cases invoked by Koscholke are such that almost all measures satisfy the suggested correct assessment. BonJour's raven example, is a case in point. Almost all measures give the result that the set consisting of "All ravens are black," "This bird is a raven," and "This bird is black" is more coherent than a set consisting of entirely unrelated propositions, in BonJour's example "This chair is brown," "Electrons are negative charged," and "Today is Thursday." Also, there is wide agreement about the normatively right answer in Bovens and Hartmann's Tweety case, which is also used as a test case. However, Koscholke notes that two measures fail to live up to the normative judgment in this case, one of them being, of course, the Glass–Olsson measure. This failure is noted as a symptom of "a general problem of the Glass–Olsson coherence measure" (p. 165). Needless to say, I now agree with this judgment: the Glass–Olsson measure is not a plausible coherence measure; it is a measure of agreement, but agreement is not a form of coherence. Surprisingly, given that it does not measure coherence, the Glass–Olsson measure agrees with the normative verdict in all other test cases (except one from Ken Akiba, which no measure complies with and for which the normative verdict can be seriously questioned).

The Shogenji measure scores much lower on the test cases, failing in five out of 10 (discounting the disputed Akiba case). The fact that the Glass–Olsson measure performs much better than the Shogenji measure vis-à-vis the test cases indicates that the former, unlike the latter, measures something that is quite close to that concept. This suggests that that "agreement," the proposed quantity measured by the Glass–Olsson measure, is conceptually closer to coherence than is "striking agreement," the proposed quantity measured by the Shogenji measure.

The conclusion of Koscholke's study is that two lesser-known measures come out on top: Meijs's generalization of the Glass–Olsson measure (Meijs, 2006) and Roche's average mutual support measure (Roche, 2013a). Both give the right result in all test cases (except the Akiba case). Both are what I will call *subset coherence measures* or subset measures, for short, because the coherence of a set is seen as a function of some measure defined on subsets of the set.

---

[33] The fact that, arguably, most examples in the literature in which two or more sets are compared vis-à-vis their relative degree of coherence involve sets of the same size might be taken as an indication that such same-size comparisons are more natural and, perhaps, more frequent than odd-size comparisons.

The Meijs coherence of a set is computed by first identifying all subsets of the set with at least two elements, then computing the Glass–Olsson coherence of each such subset, and, finally, taking the average of all these coherence values. For example, in order to compute the Meijs coherence of the extended set in the Tweety case, we first identify all subsets with at least two propositions.[34] They are:

(1) {"Tweety flies," "Tweety is a ground dweller," "Tweety is a bird"}
(2) {"Tweety flies," "Tweety is a ground dweller"}
(3) {"Tweety flies," "Tweety is a bird"}
(4) {"Tweety is a ground dweller," "Tweety is a bird"}

The next step is to determine the Glass–Olsson coherence of each of these subsets. Finally, we take the average of the resulting coherence values. We see that this is a considerably more complex measure than the original Glass–Olsson measure. Computing the Meijs coherence of a set is manageable only for small sets since the number of subsets with at least two elements grows exponentially with the size of the set.[35] The exact formula for computing Meijs coherence is given in Appendix A.

The Roche measure is intuitively even more intricate. It is based on a general recipe suggested by Douven and Meijs (2007).[36] The motivation behind this recipe is to improve on C. I. Lewis's definition of congruence. In fact, it can be seen as generalizing Lewis's definition in two respects, besides being a quantitative rather than a mere classificatory account, to use Carnap's terms. We recall that Lewis proposed to define a set as congruent if and only if each proposition in the set is supported by the other propositions in the set taken together. However, one may wonder why we should consider only single propositions and the extent to which they are supported by the rest. Why not consider how much two or more propositions and, generally, any number of the propositions are supported by the rest? Furthermore, why only consider how much they are supported by *all* the rest as opposed to how much they are supported by *some* of the rest?[37] Specifically, to compute the coherence of a given set X, we first consider all pairs Y and Z of non-empty disjoint subsets of X.

---

[34] In the examples that follow, I disregard the fact that the sets to which coherence can be meaningfully applied must be viewed as ordered sets (Bovens and Hartmann, 2003) or sets of ordered pairs (Olsson, 2005), as it is of no consequence in the present context.

[35] The considerable complexity involved in computing the Meijs coherence of larger sets of propositions is also noted in Angere (2007), p. 330. In Angere's simulations, the Meijs coherence was computed for sets of up to 15 propositions.

[36] See Douven and Meijs (2007), p 410.

[37] Douven and Meijs have a somewhat more elaborate theoretical justification for their approach. See Douven and Meijs (2007), p. 409.

For each such pair, take the conjunction of all the propositions in the set. Now compute how much the second conjunction supports the first, using some probabilistic support measure (of which there is a plentitude in the literature), and take the average. The final coherence value for X is obtained by taking the average over all these support values. The precise formula is given in Appendix A. In the case of the Rosch measure, the support measure used is obtained by taking the conditional probability: the degree to which one conjunction x is supported by another conjunction y is defined as $P(x \mid y)$.

To continue the Tweety example, the pairs of non-empty disjoint subsets in this case are:

(i)   {"Tweety flies," "Tweety is a ground dweller"} and {"Tweety is a bird"}
(i)   {"Tweety flies," "Tweety is a bird"} and {"Tweety is a ground dweller"}
(ii) {"Tweety is a ground dweller," "Tweety is a bird"} and {"Tweety flies"}
(iv) {"Tweety flies"} and {"Tweety is a ground dweller"}
(v)   {"Tweety flies"} and {"Tweety is a bird"}
(vi) {"Tweety is a ground dweller"} and {"Tweety is a bird"}

The next step is to form the conjunction of the propositions in each pair of subsets and determine the probability of the first given the other. For instance, we need to determine P("Tweety flies" $\land$ "Tweety is a ground dweller" | "Tweety is a bird"). In the final step, we take the average of the six conditional probabilities thus obtained.

The experimental study in Koscholke and Jekel (2017) further supports the conclusions in Koscholke (2016). There, for each test case, such as that involving Tweety, participants were first asked to indicate in which of the two sets the propositions fit together better or if they fit together equally well. The second task involved using a continuous slider ranging from -100 to 100 to indicate the more precise degree to which the propositions in each set fit together. Koscholke and Jekel first studied the agreement between participants' choices and the coherence assessments of each measure. The Glass–Olsson measure came out best on this score but only slightly better than the measures by Meijs and Roche. These three measures could predict 60 percent of the participants' choices. Interestingly, most measures predicted participants' choices better than chance. The authors also studied the percentage of participants who ranked propositions according to the rankings given by the measures. Again, the same three measures exceled, but so did several other measures. The Shogenji measure was found to be less capable than many other measures in predicting participants' choices. Finally, Koscholke and Jekel examined the fit between the observed coherence judgments for the different sets and coherence predictions. The Roche measure was found to perform best in this regard. Koscholke and Jekel conclude "that the participants' coherence assessments are best described by Roche's ... coherence measure" (p. 1303) and that their investigation "can be understood as providing further, empirical support for the claim that Roche's measure is a very promising candidate for an adequate probabilistic measure of coherence" (p. 1315), that is, further support in relation to, among other studies, Koscholke (2016), with which it shares the methodological limitations mentioned previously. In the next section, I will provide further reasons to disagree with Koscholke and Jekel's conclusion regarding the superiority of the Roche measure. In fact, I will raise doubts regarding the usefulness, for present epistemological purposes, of subset measures of coherence in general.

5.5 Against Subset Measures of Coherence

While the task of computing the Roche coherence for a given set of just a few propositions, given a probability distribution over those propositions, is quite easy, it quickly becomes extremely time consuming and tedious when the size of the original set grows, due to the exponential growth in the number of pairs of subsets to consider. To give a sense of the problem, consider first the Meijs measure and, as an upper bound on the complexity, the number of subsets of a given set X with n propositions $|sub(X)| = 2^n$. Hence, for a set of two propositions, $|sub(X)| = 4$. For a set of three propositions, $|sub(X)| = 8$. However, already a set of only five propositions means that there are 32 subsets to consider, not to mention the 1,024 subsets to contemplate in the case of 10 propositions. Presumably, most people would have trouble even identifying these subsets. The situation is even worse for measures, such as Roche's, that are based on the Douven and Meijs recipe, which involves considering not only a large number of subsets but also, given any one of them, a further subset of the remaining propositions among a large number of possible choices. By contrast, neither the Glass–Olsson nor the Shogenji measure is at all affected by this computational problem.

In fact, all the alternatives considered to the Glass–Olsson and Shogenji measure examined in Koscholke's and Schippers's impressive work are subset measures and are, as such, affected by the computational issue just identified. This problem does not arise in the test cases used by Koscholke (2016) and Koscholke and Jekel (2017) since the sets to compare involve at most three propositions. Nor does it arise in the study conducted by Schippers (2014a) concerning how the measures perform with respect to various proposed adequacy constraints, due to the purely theoretical nature of that study. The effect is that the competitors to Glass–Olsson and Shogenji that perform well in relation to the test cases and adequacy constraints may seem much more interesting than they in fact are.

A further case in point is Schippers (2014b). There is much to agree with in that carefully argued article. For instance, Schippers concludes, correctly, as I have explained, that striking agreement is not a form of coherence and that the Shogenji measure is therefore not a coherence measure. Thus, the fact that the Shogenji measure is reliability conducive under certain conditions does not establish it as an epistemologically fruitful concept *of coherence*. However, he also argues that what is, in effect, the Roche measure, referred to as C_A, is a measure of agreement and that it is, in a ceteris paribus sense, reliability conducive. For instance, in a scenario with two independent and initially equally credible witnesses fixing the informativeness of the propositions reported, the probability that the witnesses are reliable (truth-tellers) covaries with the degree of coherence. Schippers (p. 3675) concludes that he "has shown that by means of an agreement measure of coherence it is possible to model the relationship between coherence and reliability in a satisfactory way." More precisely, he continues, "it was shown that given a number of restrictions on witness scenarios, there is a positive correlation between coherence and reliability ceteris paribus." He proceeds to use these findings as the basis of a critique of the aforementioned argument by Schubert to the effect that the Shogenji measure can be justified as an explication of coherence because it is supposedly the only extant measure that is reliability conducive (Schippers, 2014b, p. 3676):

> However, the results in this paper demonstrate that the property of reliability conduciveness can also be modeled as a combination of coherence and specificity and, given this interpretation, that there are other measures that come out being reliability conducive. So even though I do not want to deny the fruitfulness of the Shogenji measures, it seems that there are coherence measures that are *as* fruitful and *more* similar to the explicandum. All in all, I conclude that the results proposed by Olsson and Schubert (2007) and Schubert (2011; 2012a) by no means constitute a vindication of coherence *as* striking agreement and *a fortiori* no defense of the Shogenji measure.

In the final section of his paper, Schippers returns to the justification of his agreement measure as an explication, in Carnap's sense (p. 3672):

> Only recently, Koscholke (2013) and Roche (2013[a]) proved C_A to be similar to its explicandum in a number of test cases. Beyond that, C_A is also *fruitful* as has been shown in the current paper. Needless to say, all probabilistic measures of coherence satisfy Carnap's criterion of *exactness*. Thus, there is only one of these adequacy criteria left to be considered: *simplicity*. Of course, one might argue that although the Shogenji measure is outperformed by C_A regarding *fruitfulness* and *similarity to the explicandum* and is equally exact as C_A, it is way more simple and thus preferable as an explicatum of coherence. However,

simplicity does not seem to have an intrinsic value irrespective of the other criteria. Rather, *simplicity* is a criterion in line with Occam's razor that advises to stick to simple explications given that their performance with respect to the other criteria matches the performance of complex proposals. Thus, all in all our investigation into the reliability-conduciveness of probabilistic measures of coherence corroborates C_A as an adequate explication of the notion of coherence.

There are several remarks to make at this point. It is true that simplicity is the least important requirement on an explication according to Carnap and essentially only invoked as a tiebreaker, that is, when several potential explicata of a given explicandum are equal regarding similarity, fruitfulness, and exactness. It is also true that "[t]he simplicity of a concept may be measured, in the first place, by the simplicity of the form of its definition" (1950, p. 7), and I concur that Schubert has not succeeded in justifying the Shogenji measure as an explication *of coherence*. In addition, Schippers has shown that the Roche measure (C_A) covaries with the probability of reliability if the specificity (prior probability) of the proposition reported is held fixed. Finally, the Roche measures is indeed one of the top scorers in relation to test cases and various proposed adequacy constraints, supporting its similarity with the intended explicandum (coherence). As I noted, however, the force of this observations is reduced when considering the methodological limitations of the test case approach, as it has been implemented so far in the works of Koscholke (2016) and Koscholke and Jekel (2017).

On the other hand, C_A is not only *slightly* more complex than the Shogenji (and the Glass–Olsson) measure; it is *vastly* more complex. The Shogenji measure involves computing the (prior) probability of the conjunction of the reported proposition *in one set* and dividing the result by the individual (prior) probabilities of the propositions in question. The Roche measure, by contrast, is based on the Douven–Meijs formula, which, as we saw, defines coherence as dependent on the support each non-empty subset receives from each non-empty subset of the remaining proposition in the set. Clearly, the "form of the definition," to use Carnap's expression, in the case of the Roche measure is significantly more complex than in the Shogenji case.

At this point it is pivotal not to lose sight of the internalist epistemological project in which coherentism is situated, a project that centers on the epistemic subject being able to infer the truth of believed or otherwise reported propositions, or the reliability of the processes giving rise to them, from the degree to which they cohere. This project presupposes that coherence is epistemically accessible to the subject, and more so than the properties of truth or reliability themselves. Unfortunately, the fact that calculating the Roche coherence of a given set is humanly intractable for even modestly large sets of propositions raises serious doubts precisely about the epistemic accessibility of coherence in this sense.[38]

Hence, although the Roche measure does have its advantages, it is considerably less attractive – indeed, perhaps not attractive at all – for epistemological purposes. If, as Schippers suggests, the most plausible candidate for an explication of coherence is a subset measure, this is in fact (more) bad news for the coherentist because it means that coherence is epistemically inaccessible. Otherwise put, it would show not that coherence is not definable, which was our earlier conclusion in connection with truth-conduciveness and the definition problem and one reason why we turned to Carnap's method of explication in the first place, but that coherence, for the epistemological purposes that we are here interested in, is not even explicable. I will refer to this problem, accordingly, as that of *epistemic access*.

It might be objected that even if there are computational difficulties with the Roche measure, its performance in test cases, such as those investigated by Koscholke, is still quite suggestive. Somehow it manages to track our intuitive assessments of coherence in many cases. However, it should be borne in mind that those test cases concern sets with just two or three propositions. As far as I know, the verdicts of subset measures have never been compared to intuitive judgment for larger sets of propositions. In fact, it is difficult to see what intuitive quality they would track, except perhaps a general, vague sense of everything one believes being, wholly and partly, connected. I will return to this point in what follows. This is not so for the Glass–Olsson and Shogenji measures. The former, as I noted, tracks the intuitive quality of standing or falling together; propositions in a set that is highly Glass–Olsson coherent are likely to be either true together or false together. The latter tracks the intuitive quality of "striking agreement that suggests an explanation other than chance." That we should have evolved heuristics for assessing these qualities, even for larger sets, does not seem excessively unlikely.

The situation is similar regarding the common assumption in the coherentist literature that a coherent set be logically consistent, exemplified, for instance, in the works of A. C. Ewing and Laurence BonJour. Regarding consistency, too, it

---

[38] Jacob Koscholke (2016) has developed software that automatically computes the Roche coherence, or the coherence according to other subset measures, of a given set. In modern life, computers effortlessly do much of the work that was previously carried out by humans, so why not delegate the computation of the Roche coherence of one's beliefs to a computer? It is at present unclear whether this would solve the problem for realistic sets of beliefs since a systematic complexity study seems to be lacking. For all we know, the task may quickly become too complex even for a computer.

has been argued that checking for it would be, in general, computationally intractable. Hilary Kornblith has emphasized this point (Kornblith, 1989), p. 211:

> It is not simply that human beings have difficulty in determining the consistency of large sets of sentences. It is simply beyond the powers of any possible computational device to determine the consistency of a large set of sentences.

For instance, checking the consistency of a set of propositions containing 10 propositional variables by the truth table method would require a table with $2^{10} = 1024$ lines – as we saw, a number on the same magnitude as the number of subsets to be considered in the computation of the coherence of a set containing 10 propositions according to many subset measures.

The epistemological inaccessibility of consistency can also be supported by reference to Church's theorem for the undecidability of predicate logic and Gödel's second theory for the general unprovability of consistency (Halbach, 2003, p. 79). The former shows that there is no exact procedure for determining whether a given set of sentences is or is not consistent in predicate logic, the latter that no system satisfying some minimal requirements can prove its own consistency. Volker Halbach (ibid.) concludes that the jury is still out regarding the question whether consistency is an epistemically accessible property in the sense required by coherentism. It seems to me that the same is true mutatis mutandis regarding the Roche measure and other subset measures: these measures unfortunately place coherence, in the sense of mutual support, on a par with consistency in terms of computational complexity and epistemic access.

A related problem is that of determining the probabilities involved in candidate measures of coherence. I will refer to this problem as the *problem of probability assessment*. In the Shogenji and Glass–Olsson cases, only a few probabilities need to be assessed for the definition to be employed in a concrete case. For the latter, we need to assess the probability that all propositions are true and the probability that at least one of them is, before the propositions were reported. Returning to the case with Bert, this would be the prior probability that Bert was at the crime scene *and* has the same type of gun *and* deposited a large sum of money the next day, as well as the prior probability that at least one of these propositions is true. The prior probability that Bert would own the same type of gun will depend on how common that type of gun is in the relevant population. The prior probability that he would be at the crime scene will depend on where Bert lives and works, and so on. In many cases, it would be nontrivial to assess even the two probabilities referred to in the definition of the Glass–Olsson measure with some confidence. For subset measures and sets of even modest size, there is a much larger number of unconditional or conditional probabilities to determine. Thus, from a certain size, subset measures are much more affected by the probability assessment problem than the Shogenji or Glass–Olsson measures.

Finally, I will question subset measures on intuitive grounds. The idea behind subset measures is, roughly, that for a set to be coherent in the sense of forming a unified whole, it is not enough that it itself exhibits that property; so must all its parts. Yet, it seems to me that this requirement goes beyond the intuitive meaning of the concept. This gives rise to a final problem that I propose to call the *problem of excessive support*. For instance, an artwork may be a unified whole even though its parts are not unified wholes. After all, the different parts of a painting do not usually qualify as artworks in their own right. The analogue of the Douven–Meijs recipe for art would be an esthetical theory that requires of a magnificent, coherent piece of art that its parts are also magnificent and coherent. On this theory, a novel can be a great unified work only if each chapter, indeed each section of a chapter, is itself a great unified work. This requirement excludes artworks that cannot be appreciated except in their entirety, such as a novel in which the events appear fragmentary and unconnected until the very last chapter, or the very last section or even sentence, where, finally, everything falls into place. Another possible counterexample would be conceptual art. On the theory in question, a piece of conceptual art consisting of a guiding concept and its physical implementation (a painting, a piece of music, et cetera) is highly coherent only if it remains highly coherent when stripped of the concept. But this cannot be right. Consider, for example, John Cage's *4′33″* in which the performer is asked to do nothing for 4 minutes and 33 seconds, the concept behind it being, reportedly, that any sound, or absence thereof, may constitute music. For it to be unified work, on this model, the physical part of it – the 4 minutes and 33 seconds of silence – must also be a unified, esthetically pleasing whole. Yet, if conceptual art is stripped of the concept, there is a sense in which nothing (in John Cage's case, literally nothing) remains.[39]

To take a scientific example of a unified whole that does not have unified parts, consider the case of several previously unconnected phenomena being unified by one overarching theory. This is hailed as a great achievement because

---

[39] Angere (2007) considers a similar argument (p. 332): "the important thing is how the set of all beliefs as a whole hangs together, and not how the subsets of it do. The justification of smaller subsets as well as individual beliefs proceeds downward from the full set. Strictly speaking, the coherence of these does not matter at all."

of the unification thus achieved. In a seminal paper, Friedman (1974), pp. 14–15, takes the kinetic theory of gases as an illustration:

> The kinetic theory of gases effects a significant *unification* in what we have to accept. Where we once had three independent brute facts – that gases approximately obey the Boyle–Charles law, that they obey Graham's law, and that they have the specific-heat capacities they do have – we now have only one – that molecules obey the laws of mechanics.

Clearly, scientists in the field would agree with Friedman that the set *X* consisting of the kinetic theory of gases together with these three "independent brute facts" is a highly, perhaps maximally, coherent set. On a subset measure of coherence along the lines of Douven and Meijs, this would mean that any subset of this set is supported by any subset of the remaining set. Consider, however, a subset of *X* consisting of two of the brute facts, say, that gases approximately obey the Boyle–Charles law and Graham's law. Among the non-empty, disjoint subsets of the remaining propositions in *X* we have the fact that gases have the specific-heat capacities that they have. Now, by assumption, the latter set does not support the former. The same is true for other ways of partitioning the three brute facts into non-empty disjoint subsets: the resulting sets (or their conjunctions) will not confer support on each other. Hence, on the Douven–Meijs recipe, Friedman's paradigm case of a unified scientific whole would not come out as very coherent at all. Furthermore, in contrast to what that recipe implies, the degree of unification would have been lower, not higher, had the facts explained been dependent and mutually supporting in the absence of the kinetic theory. It is, after all, the fact that *independent* phenomena could be brought under the same theoretical umbrella that made the whole highly coherent.

6 Conclusion

It is time to sum up the preceding discussion, and to bring out some further conclusions. In the light of the results established in the aftermath of the probabilistic turn in coherentist epistemology, most researchers have concluded that the coherence of a set of statements constitutes a reason to believe in the joint truth of those statements, provided that the reporters are partially reliable and collectively independent. The precise probability thus attained depends on the individual reliability of the reporters and on the probability of the statements prior to being reported. Thus, a pure form of coherentism that does not require partial reliability on behalf of the reporters can be safely excluded from further consideration. This insight affects the coherentist's response to the radical skeptic in destructive ways. For the coherentist must assume that the mechanisms behind the formation of her empirical beliefs satisfy the conditions of partial reliability and independence. Yet, any beliefs to these effects would themselves be empirical and therefore part of the very system whose justification is in question. Attempts to justify the assumption of partial reliability on a priori grounds were seen to fail. The upshot was that reference to the high degree of coherence of the totality of our beliefs could at best point to their actual truth being an interesting hypothesis for further consideration.

Another fundamental result in the probabilistic study of coherence – the impossibility theorem – revealed that no account of coherence can be truth-conducive in the sense of higher coherence implying a higher likelihood of joint truth, not even under the conditions of partial reliability and independence and in a weak ceteris paribus sense. In response, many authors, myself included, proposed, as I explained at some length, other ways of conceiving the connection between coherence and truth, such as reliability conduciveness or relaxing the connection to a mere statistical relation, and it turned out that these alternative accounts often put the Glass–Olsson as well as the Shogenji measure of coherence in a favorable light. Even so, both measures fall prey to counter-examples showing that they fail as conceptual analyses of the target concept.

The resulting somewhat perplexing situation suggested another methodological approach, namely, that of explication, in Rudolf Carnap's sense. Having explained the basic ideas, I turned to the recent discussion of coherence measures as explications. In this connection, I raised serious doubts regarding the epistemological usefulness of the main alternatives to the Glass–Olsson and Shogenji measures, namely, measures that, roughly speaking, consider the coherence not only of the whole but also of its parts. My criticism of such subset measures focused on problems of epistemic access (computational complexity), probability assessment, and excessive support. The Glass–Olsson and Shogenji measures were seen to be largely unaffected by these problems. However, neither strictly speaking measures coherence, as opposed to agreement (Glass–Olsson) and striking agreement (Shogenji). Even so, the Glass–Olsson measure, surprisingly, complies with a selection of test cases designed for coherence measures considered so far, and it also performs very well in predicting laymen's intuitive coherence judgments in relation to these cases. Thus, what it measures is likely to be closely related to coherence, even if it fails to coincide with that concept. This is arguably to a lesser extent the case for the Shogenji measure. My tentative and qualified conclusion is therefore that while both measures are useful in relation to Carnap's requirements on an explication, the Glass–Olsson measure stands out as the one that comes closest to satisfying the coherence theorist's particular epistemological demands.

Appendix A: Proposed Measures of Coherence

This appendix provides formal definitions of the candidate measures of coherence that have been most extensively studied in the recent literature on epistemic coherence (e.g. Koscholke, 2016; Koscholke and Jekel, 2017; Schippers, 2014a). The notation has been adopted from Koscholke (2016).

The Glass–Olsson measure (Glass, 2002; Olsson, 2002c):

$$C_{go}(X) = \frac{P\left(\wedge_{i=1}^{n} x_i\right)}{P\left(\vee_{i=1}^{n} x_i\right)}.$$

The Shogenji measure (Shogenji, 1999):

$$C_{sho}(X) = \frac{P\left(\overset{n}{\underset{i=1}{\wedge}} x_i\right)}{\prod_{i=1}^{n} P(x_i)}.$$

An alternative generalization of the idea behind the Glass–Olsson measure was suggested by Meijs (2006):

$$C_{mei}(X) = \frac{\sum_{i=1}^{(2^n - n)-1} C_{go}(X_i')}{(2^n - n) - 1}.$$

The Meijs coherence of a set X is the average Glass–Olsson coherence of all subsets of X with at least two propositions.

Schupbach (2011) proposed an alternative generalization of the idea behind the Shogenji measure:

$$C_{sch}(X) = \frac{\sum_{j=2}^{n} \dfrac{\sum_{i=1}^{\binom{n}{j}} \log\left(C_{sho}\left(X_{ij}'\right)\right)}{\binom{n}{j}}}{n - 1}.$$

Roughly, the Schupbach coherence of X is the average Shogenji coherence of all subsets of X with at least two propositions.

Douven and Mejis (2007) suggested a general recipe for generating coherence measures from measures of support, that is, functions indicating how much the first proposition is supported by the second:

$$C_S(X) = \frac{\sum_{i=1}^{(3^n - 2^{n+1}) - 1} S\left(\left(\bigwedge_{x_j \in X'} x_j, \bigwedge_{x_k \in X''} x_k\right)_i\right)}{(3^n - 2^{n+1}) - 1}.$$

To compute the Douven and Mejis coherence of X with respect to a support measure S, consider all pairs of non-empty, disjoint subsets of X. For each such pair, take the conjunctions over the propositions contained in the sets and calculate the degree of support the first set received from the second according to S. Finally, take the average of all these values.

The Douvens and Mejis recipe has been applied to many support measures, including the measures listed in the following.

The Fitelson measure (Fitelson, 2003):

$$S_{fit}(x_1, x_2) = \begin{cases} \dfrac{P(x_2|x_1) - P(x_2|\neg x_1)}{P(x_2|x_1) + P(x_2|\neg x_1)} & \text{if } x_2 \nvdash x_1 \text{ and } x_2 \nvdash \neg x_1 \\ 1 & \text{if } x_2 \vdash x_1 \text{ and } x_2 \nvdash \neg \bot \,. \\ -1 & \text{if } x_2 \vdash \neg x_1 \end{cases}$$

Carnap's first (difference) measure (Carnap, 1950):

$$S_{car}(x_1, x_2) = P(x_1|x_2) - P(x_1).$$

Carnap's second (relevance) measure (Carnap, 1950):

$$S_{car'}(x_1, x_2) = P(x_1 \wedge x_2) - P(x_1) \cdot P(x_2).$$

Keynes's measure (Keynes, 1921):

$$S_{key}(x_1, x_2) = \frac{P(x_1|x_2)}{P(x_1)}.$$

Good's measure (Good, 1984):

$$S_{goo}(x_1, x_2) = \frac{P(x_2|x_1)}{P(x_2|\neg x_1)}.$$

Roche's measure (Roche, 2013a):

$$S_{roc}(x_1, x_2) = \begin{cases} P(x_1|x_2) & \text{if } x_2 \nvdash x_1 \text{ and } x_2 \nvdash \neg x_1 \\ 1 & \text{if } x_2 \vdash x_1 \text{ and } x_2 \nvdash \bot \,. \\ 0 & \text{if } x_2 \vdash \neg x_1 \end{cases}$$

Schippers's measure (Schippers, 2014a):

$$S_{sch}(x_1, x_2) = \begin{cases} \dfrac{P(x_1|x_2) - P(x_1|\neg x_2)}{1 - P(x_1|\neg x_2)} & \text{if } P(x_1|x_2) \geq P(x_1) \\ \dfrac{P(x_1|x_2) - P(x_1|\neg x_2)}{P(x_1|\neg x_2)} & \text{if } P(x_1|x_2) < P(x_1) \end{cases}.$$

Nozick's measure (Nozick, 1981):

$$S_{noz}(x_1, x_2) = P(x_2|x_1) - P(x_2|\neg x_1).$$

Popper's measure (1954):

$$S_{pop}(x_1, x_2) = \frac{P(x_2|x_1) - P(x_2)}{P(x_2|x_1) + P(x_2)} \cdot (1 + P(x_1) \cdot P(x_1|x_2)).$$

Rescher's measure (1958):

$$S_{res}(x_1, x_2) = \frac{P(x_1|x_2) - P(x_1)}{1 - P(x_1)} \cdot P(x_2).$$

The measure by Crupi, Tentori, and Gonzales (2007):

$$S_{cru}(x_1, x_2) = \begin{cases} \dfrac{P(x_1|x_2) - P(x_1)}{1 - P(x_1)} & \text{if } P(x_1|x_2) \geq P(x_1) \\ \dfrac{P(x_1|x_2) - P(x_1)}{P(x_1)} & \text{if } P(x_1|x_2) < P(x_1) \end{cases}.$$

Gaifman's measure (Gaifman, 1979):

$$Sgai(x_1, x_2) = \frac{P(\neg x_1)}{P(\neg x_1|x_2)}.$$

Rips's measure (Rips, 2001):

$$S_{rip}(x_1, x_2) = 1 - \frac{P(\neg x_2|x_1)}{P(\neg x_2)}.$$

Finally, Shogenji's proposed measure of justification has been employed as a support measure:

$$S_{sho}(x_1, x_2) = \frac{\log_2 P(x_1|x_2) - \log_2 P(x_1)}{-\log_2 P(x_1)}.$$

Appendix B: Proposed Test Cases for Measures of Coherence

The focus of much of the recent discussion of the adequacy of coherence measures has been on 11 proposed test cases (e.g. Koscholke, 2016; Koscholke and Jekel, 2017; Schippers, 2014a).

Akiba's Die Case

Imagine tossing a fair die and consider the following three predictions about the outcome:

x_1: The die will come up 2.
x_2: The die will come up 2 or 4.
x_3: The die will come up 2 or 4 or 6.

According to Akiba (2000), the sets $\{x_1, x_2\}$ and $\{x_1, x_3\}$ should be equal with respect to their degrees of coherence since both x_2 and x_3 are deductive consequences of x_1.

BonJour's Raven Case

Situation 1:
$x_{1.1}$: All ravens are black.
$x_{1.2}$: This bird is a raven.
$x_{1.3}$: This bird is black.

Situation 2:
$x_{2.1}$: This chair is brown.
$x_{2.2}$: Electrons are negatively charged.
$x_{2.3}$: Today is Thursday.

Since the set $\{x_{1.1}, x_{1.2}, x_{1.3}\}$ consists of propositions that are related by relevance and entailment, whereas the propositions in $\{x_{2.1}, x_{2.2}, x_{2.3}\}$ have nothing to do with each other, the first set is, according to BonJour (1985), more coherent than the second.

Bovens and Hartmann's Tweety Case

Situation 1:
$x_{1.1}$: Tweety is a bird.
$x_{1.2}$: Tweety is a ground dweller.

Situation 2:

$x_{2.1}$: Tweety is a bird.

$x_{2.2}$: Tweety is a ground dweller.

$x_{2.3}$: Tweety is a penguin.

According to Bovens and Hartmann (2003), the set $\{x_{2.1}, x_{2.2}, x_{2.3}\}$ is more coherent than the set $\{x_{1.1}, x_{1.2}\}$ since, given our background knowledge about penguins, the information that Tweety is a penguin entails that Tweety is a bird and allows us to inductively infer that Tweety is a ground dweller.

Bovens and Hartmann's Tokyo Murder Case

A murder has occurred in Tokyo, but the corpse has not been found yet. Imagine a grid over the map of the city consisting of 100 numbered squares with each square having the same probability of being the location the corpse is to be found. Two witnesses give their reports about the location of the corpse. Notation: $x_{i,j}$ is the report of witness j in situation i.

Situation 1:

$x_{1.1}$: The corpse is in squares 50–60.

$x_{1.2}$: The corpse is in squares 51–61.

Situation 2:

$x_{2.1}$: The corpse is in squares 22–55.

$x_{2.2}$: The corpse is in squares 55–90.

Situation 3:

$x_{3.1}$: The corpse is in squares 20–61.

$x_{3.2}$: The corpse is in squares 50–91.

Situation 4:

$x_{4.1}$: The corpse is in squares 41–60.

$x_{4.2}$: The corpse is in squares 51–70.

Situation 5:

$x_{5.1}$: The corpse is in squares 39–61.

$x_{5.2}$: The corpse is in squares 50–72.

In Bovens and Hartmann's view, $\{x_{1.1}, x_{1.2}\}$ is more coherent than either $\{x_{2.1}, x_{2.2}\}$ or $\{x_{3.1}, x_{3.2}\}$. The coherence of $\{x_{4.1}, x_{4.2}\}$ and $\{x_{5.1}, x_{5.2}\}$ should be similar (Bovens and Hartmann, 2003).

Bovens and Hartmann's Culprit Case

Imagine that we want to identify the culprit in a murder case. Three witnesses give their reports, where $x_{i,j}$ is the report of witness j in situation i.

Situation 1:
$x_{1.1}$: The culprit was a woman.
$x_{1.2}$: The culprit had a Danish accent.
$x_{1.3}$: The culprit drove a Ford.

Situation 2:
$x_{2.1}$: The culprit wore Coco Chanel shoes.
$x_{2.2}$: The culprit had a French accent.
$x_{2.3}$: The culprit drove a Renault.

Situation 3:
$x_{3.1}$: The culprit wore Coco Chanel shoes.
$x_{3.2}$: The culprit had a French accent.
$x_{3.3}$: The culprit drove a Ford.

According to Bovens and Hartmann (2003), $\{x_{2.1}, x_{2.2}, x_{2.3}\}$ is more coherent than $\{x_{1.1}, x_{1.2}, x_{1.3}\}$ since the reports fit together better in the former than they do in the latter. They suspend judgment with respect to $\{x_{3.1}, x_{3.2}, x_{3.3}\}$.

Glass's Dodecahedron Case

Situation 1: A fair die is rolled. Consider the following predictions:

$x_{1.1}$: The die will come up 2.
$x_{1.2}$: The die will come up 2 or 4.

Situation 2: A fair dodecahedron is rolled. Consider the following predictions:

$x_{2.1}$: The dodecahedron will come up 2.
$x_{2.2}$: The dodecahedron will come up 2 or 4.

According to Glass (2005), $\{x_{1.1}, x_{1.2}\}$ and $\{x_{2.1}, x_{2.2}\}$ are equally coherent.

Meijs's Samurai Sword Case

Imagine that a murder occurred in a big city and we are interested in finding the murderer.
Situation 1: There are ten million independent and equally likely suspects. 1,059 suspects are Japanese, 1,059 suspects own a Samurai sword, and nine suspects

are Japanese and own a Samurai sword. Consider the following two propositions:

$x_{1.1}$: The murderer is Japanese.
$x_{1.2}$: The murderer owns a Samurai sword.

Situation 2: There are 100 independent and equally likely suspects. Ten suspects are Japanese, ten suspects own a Samurai sword, and nine suspects are Japanese and own a Samurai sword. Consider the following two propositions:

$x_{2.1}$: The murderer is Japanese.
$x_{2.2}$: The murderer owns a Samurai sword.

According to Meijs, $\{x_{1.1}, x_{1.2}\}$ is less coherent than $\{x_{2.1}, x_{2.2}\}$.

Meijs' Albino Rabbit Case

Imagine a population of 102 rabbits living on an island and consider the following two situations:
Situation 1: 101 rabbits are grey, 101 rabbits have two ears, and 100 rabbits are grey and have two ears. Randomly pick one of the rabbits and consider the following two propositions:

$x_{1.1}$: The rabbit is grey.
$x_{1.2}$: The rabbit has two ears.

Situation 2: 100 rabbits are grey, 100 rabbits have two ears, and 100 rabbits are grey and have two ears. Randomly pick one of the rabbits and consider the same two propositions:

$x_{2.1}$: The rabbit is grey.
$x_{2.2}$: The rabbit has two ears.

According to Meijs (2006), $\{x_{1.1}, x_{1.2}\}$ is less coherent than $\{x_{2.1}, x_{2.2}\}$.

Meijs and Douven's Plane Lottery Case

Kate participates in a lottery. The test case is described as follows in Koscholke (2016), p. 173:

> She enters a windowless plane that either flies to the North Pole, the South Pole or New Zealand. Kate's chances are as follows: 4/100 for flying to the North Pole, 49/100 for flying to the South Pole and 47/100 for flying to New Zealand. The probability of seeing a penguin given she is on the South Pole is 10/49, given she is in New Zealand is 1/47 and given she is on the North Pole is 0. Suppose

that after the random flight Kate leaves the plane not knowing where she has landed. She faces two equally reliable people and an animal she is unable to recognize.

Two people give their reports. Consider the following situations:

Situation 1:
$x_{1.1}$: The animal you see is a penguin.
$x_{1.2}$: You are on the North Pole.

Situation 2:
$x_{2.1}$: The animal you see is a penguin.
$x_{2.2}$: You are on the South Pole.

According to Meijs and Douven (2005), $\{x_{1.1}, x_{1.2}\}$ is less coherent than $\{x_{2.1}, x_{2.2}\}$.

Schupbach's Robber Case

Imagine eight suspects, each having the same probability of having committed a robbery. Three witnesses give their reports. Consider the following situations.

Situation 1:
$x_{1.1}$: The robbery was committed by suspects 1, 2, or 3.
$x_{1.2}$: The robbery was committed by suspects 1, 2, or 4.
$x_{1.3}$: The robbery was committed by suspects 1, 3, or 4.

Situation 2:
$x_{2.1}$: The robbery was committed by suspects 1, 2, or 3.
$x_{2.2}$: The robbery was committed by suspects 1, 4, or 5.
$x_{2.3}$: The robbery was committed by suspects 1, 6, or 7.

According to Schupbach, $\{x_{1.1}, x_{1.2}, x_{1.3}\}$ is more coherent than $\{x_{2.1}, x_{2.2}, x_{2.3}\}$.

Siebel's Pickpocketing Robber Case

There are ten independent and equally likely suspects for a murder. Eight suspects committed a robbery, eight suspects committed a pickpocketing, and six committed both. Consider the following two propositions:

x_1: The murderer committed a robbery.
x_2: The murderer committed a pickpocketing.

According to Siebel (2004), the set $\{x_{1.1}, x_{1.2}\}$ is not incoherent.

References

Akiba, K. (2000), "Shogenji's Probabilistic Measure of Coherence Is Incoherent," Analysis, 60 (4): 356–359.

Alston, W. P. (1993), "Epistemic Desiderata," Philosophy and Phenomenological Research, 53 (3): 527–551.

Angere, S. (2007), "The Defeasible Nature of Coherentist Justification," Synthese, 157 (3): 321–335.

Angere, S. (2008), "Coherence as a Heuristic," Mind, 117 (465): 1–26.

Baumann, P. (2016), Epistemic Contextualism: A Defense, Oxford: Oxford University Press.

Blanshard, B. (1939), The Nature of Thought, London: Allen & Unwin.

BonJour, L. (1985), The Structure of Empirical Knowledge, Cambridge, MA: Harvard University Press.

Bovens, L., and Hartmann, S. (2003), Bayesian Epistemology, Oxford: Clarendon Press.

Bovens, L., and Olsson, E. J. (2000), "Coherentism, Reliability and Bayesian Networks," Mind, 109 (436): 685–719.

Bovens, L., and Olsson, E. J. (2002), "Believing More, Risking Less: On Coherence, Truth and Non-trivial Extensions," Erkenntnis, 57 (2): 137–150.

Bovens, L., Fitelson, B., Hartmann, S., and Snyder, J. (2002), "Too Odd (Not) to Be True? A Reply to Olsson," British Journal for the Philosophy of Science, 53 (4): 539–563.

Carnap, R. (1950), Logical Foundations of Probability, Chicago: Chicago University Press.

Chisholm, R. M. (1977), Theory of Knowledge (2nd ed.), Englewood Cliffs, NJ: Prentice-Hall.

Coady, C. A. J. (1992), Testimony: A Philosophical Study, Clarendon Press: Oxford.

Cordes, M., and Siegwart, G. (2019), "Explication," in The Internet Encyclopedia of Philosophy. Accessed August 20, 2019 at www.iep.utm.edu/explicat.

Cross, C. B. (1999), "Coherence and Truth Conducive Justification," Analysis, 59 (3): 186–193.

Crupi, V., Tentori, K., and Gonzales, M. (2007), "On Bayesian Measures of Evidential Support: Theoretical and Empirical Issues," Philosophy of Science, 74 (2): 229–252.

Davidson, D. (1986), "A Coherence Theory of Knowledge and Truth," in Truth and Interpretation, E. LePore (ed.), Oxford: Blackwell, pp. 307–319.

Dietrich, F., and Moretti, L. (2005), "On Coherent Sets and the Transmission of Confirmation," Philosophy of Science, 72 (3): 403–424.

Douven, I., and Meijs, W. (2007), "Measuring Coherence," Synthese, 156 (3): 405–425.

Ewing, A. C. (1934), Idealism: A Critical Survey, London: Methuen.

Fitelson, B. (2003), "A Probabilistic Theory of Coherence," Analysis, 63 (3): 194–199.

Friedman, M. (1974), "Explanation and Scientific Understanding," The Journal of Philosophy, 11 (1): 5–19.

Gaifman, H. (1979), "Subjective Probability, Natural Predicates and Hempel's Ravens," Erkenntnis, 14 (2): 105–147.

Glass, D. H. (2002), "Coherence, Explanation and Bayesian Networks," in Artificial Intelligence and Cognitive Science, M. O'Neill and R. F. E. Sutcliffe et al. (eds.) (Lecture Notes in Artificial Intelligence, vol. 2464), Berlin: Springer-Verlag, pp. 177–182.

Glass, D. H. (2005), "Problems with Priors in Probabilistic Measures of Coherence," Erkenntnis, 63 (3): 375–385.

Glass, D. H. (2007), "Coherence Measures and Inference to the Best Explanation," Synthese, 157 (3): 257–296.

Goldman, A. I. (1979), "What Is Justified Belief?", in Justification and Knowledge, G. Pappas (ed.), Boston: D. Reidel, pp. 1–25.

Goldman, A. I. (1999), Knowledge in a Social World, New York: Oxford University Press.

Good, I. J. (1984), "The Best Explicatum for Weight of Evidence," Journal of Statistical Computation and Simulation, 19: 294–299.

Haack, S. (2009), Evidence and Inquiry: A Pragmatist Reconstruction of Epistemology, Amherst, NY: Prometheus Books.

Halbach, V. (2003), "Can We Grasp Consistency?", in The Epistemology of Keith Lehrer, E. J. Olsson (ed.), Philosophical Studies Series, 95, Dordrecht: Kluwer Academic Publishers, pp. 75–87.

Harris, A. J. L., and Hahn, U. (2009), "Bayesian Rationality in Evaluating Multiple Testimonies: Incorporating the Role of Coherence," Journal of Experimental Psychology: Learning, Memory, and Cognition, 35 (5): 1366–1372.

Hendricks, V. F. (2006), Mainstream and Formal Epistemology, New York: Cambridge University Press.

Hilpinen, R. (1991), "Inquiry, Argumentation and Knowledge," in The Logic of Theory Change, A. Fuhrmann and M. Morreau (eds.), Lecture Notes in Computer Science (Lecture Notes in Artificial Intelligence), vol. 465. Berlin and Heidelberg: Springer, pp. 1–18.

Huemer, M. (1997), "Probability and Coherence Justification," Southern Journal of Philosophy, 35 (4): 463–472.

Huemer, M. (2007), "Weak Bayesian Coherentism," Synthese, 157 (3): 337–346.

Huemer, M. (2011), "Does Probability Theory Refute Coherentism?", Journal of Philosophy, 108 (1): 35–54.

Kemeny, J., and Oppenheim, P. (1952), "Degree of Factual Support," Philosophy of Science, 19 (4): 307–324.

Keynes, J. (1921), A Treatise on Probability, London: Macmillan.

Klein, P., and Warfield, T. A. (1994), "What Price Coherence?", Analysis, 54 (3): 129–132.

Klein, P., and Warfield, T. A. (1996), "No Help for the Coherentist," Analysis, 56 (2): 118–121.

Kornblith, H. (1989), "The Unattainability of Coherence," in The Current State of the Coherence Theory, J. Bender (ed.), Dordrecht: Kluwer Academic Publishers, pp. 207–214.

Koscholke, J. (2013), "Last Measure Standing: Evaluating Test Cases for Probabilistic Coherence Measures," unpublished manuscript.

Koscholke, J. (2016), "Evaluating Test Cases of Probabilistic Measures of Coherence," Erkenntnis, 81: 155–181.

Koscholke, J., and Jekel, M. (2017), "Probabilistic Coherence Measures: A Psychological Study of Coherence Assessment," Synthese, published online January 11, 2016, doi: https://doi.org/10.1007/s11229-015-0996-6.

Koscholke, J., and Schippers, M. (2016), "Against Relative Overlap Measures of Coherence," Synthese, first online September 15, 2015, doi: https://doi.org/10.1007/s11229-015-0887-x.

Koscholke, J., Schippers, M., and Stegman, A. (2019), "New Hope for Relative Overlap Measures of Coherence," Mind, 128 (512): 1261–1284.

Lehrer, K. (1990), Theory of Knowledge, 1st ed., Boulder, CO: Westview Press.

Lewis, C. I. (1946), An Analysis of Knowledge and Valuation, LaSalle, IL: Open Court.

Lycan, W. G. (1988), Judgment and Justification, New York: Cambridge University Press.

Lycan, W. G. (2002), "Explanation and Epistemology," in The Oxford Handbook of Epistemology, P. K. Moser (ed.), New York: Oxford University Press, pp. 408–433.

Lycan, W. G. (2012), "Explanationist Rebuttals (Coherentism Defended Again)," The Southern Journal of Philosophy, 50 (1): 5–20.

Meijs, W. (2006), "Coherence as Generalized Logical Equivalence," Erkenntnis, 64 (2): 231–252.

Meijs, W., and Douven, I. (2005), "Bovens and Hartmann on Coherence," Mind, 114 (454): 355–363.

Meijs, W., and Douven, I. (2007), "On the Alleged Impossibility of Coherence," Synthese, 157 (3): 347–360.

Moretti, L. (2007), "Ways in Which Coherence Is Confirmation Conducive," Synthese, 157 (3): 309–319.

Moretti, L., and Akiba, K. (2007), "Probabilistic Measures of Coherence and the Problem of Belief Individuation," Synthese, 154 (1): 73–95.

Nozick, R. (1981), Philosophical Explanations, Oxford: Clarendon Press.

Olsson, E. J. (2001), "Why Coherence Is Not Truth-Conducive," Analysis, 61 (3): 236–241.

Olsson, E. J. (2002a), "Corroborating Testimony, Probability and Surprise," British Journal for the Philosophy of Science, 53 (2): 273–288.

Olsson, E. J. (2002b), "Corroborating Testimony and Ignorance: A Reply to Bovens, Fitelson, Hartmann and Snyder," British Journal for the Philosophy of Science, 53 (4): 565–572.

Olsson, E. J. (2002c), "What Is the Problem of Coherence and Truth?", The Journal of Philosophy, 99 (5): 246–272.

Olsson, E. J. (2005), Against Coherence: Truth, Probability, and Justification, Oxford: Clarendon Press.

Olsson, E. J. (2015), "Gettier and the Method of Explication: a 60 Year Old Solution to a 50 Year Old Problem," Philosophical Studies 172 (1), 1: 57–72.

Olsson, E. J. (2017a), "Explicationist Epistemology and Epistemic Pluralism," in Epistemic Pluralism, A. Coliva and N. J. L. L. Pedersen (eds.), Palgrave Macmillian, pp. 23–46.

Olsson, E. J. (2017b), "Coherentism," in Routledge Handbook of Philosophy of Memory, S. Bernecker and K. Michaelian (eds.), New York: Routledge, pp. 310–322.

Olsson, E. J. (2021a), Kunskapsteori: En Historisk och Systematisk Introduktion, Lund: Studentlitteratur AB.

Olsson, E. J. (2021b), "Coherentist Theories of Epistemic Justification," The Stanford Encyclopedia of Philosophy (Fall 2021 Edition), Edward N. Zalta (ed.), https://plato.stanford.edu/archives/fall2021/entries/justep-coherence.

Olsson, E. J. (2022), "Hilpinen's Theory of Inquiry," in Agency, Norms, Inquiry, and Artifacts: Essays in Honor of Risto Hilpinen, P. McNamara et al. (eds.), Synthese Library 454, 175–191.

Olsson, E. J., and Schubert, S. (2007), "Reliability Conducive Measures of Coherence," Synthese, 157 (3): 297–308.

Pearl, J. (1988), Probabilistic Reasoning in Intelligent Systems: Networks of Plausible Inference, San Francisco: Morgan Kaufmann Publishers.

Popper, K. R. (1954), "Degree of Confirmation," British Journal for the Philosophy of Science, 5 (18), 143–149.

Quine, W. and Ullian, J. (1970), The Web of Belief, New York: Random House.

Rescher, N. (1958), "Theory of Evidence," Philosophy of Science, 25 (1), 83–94.

Rescher, N. (1973), The Coherence Theory of Truth, Oxford: Oxford University Press.

Rips, L. J. (2001), "Two Kinds of Reasoning," Psychological Science, 12 (2), 129–134.

Roche, W. (2010), "Coherentism, Truth, and Witness Agreement," Acta Analytica, 25 (2): 243–257.

Roche, W. (2013a), "Coherence and Probability: A Probabilistic Account of Coherence," In M. Araszkiewicz & J. Savelka (eds.), Coherence: Insights from Philosophy, Jurisprudence and Artificial Intelligence (pp. 59–91). Dordrecht: Springer.

Roche, W. (2013b), "On the Truth-Conduciveness of Coherence," Erkenntnis, 79 (S3): 1–19.

Schippers, M. (2014a), "Probabilistic Measures of Coherence: From Adequacy Constraints Towards Pluralism," Synthese, 191 (16): 3821–3845.

Schippers, M. (2014b), "Incoherence and Inconsistency," Review of Symbolic Logic, 7 (3), 511–528.

Schippers, M., and Siebel, M. (2015), "Inconsistency as a Touchstone for Coherence Measures," Theoria: Revista de Teoria, Historia y Fundamentos de la Ciencia, 30 (1): 11–41.

Schubert, S. (2011), "Coherence and Reliability: The Case of Overlapping Testimonies," Erkenntnis, 74 (2), 263–275.

Schubert, S. (2012a), "Coherence Reasoning and Reliability: A Defense of the Shogenji Measure," Synthese, 187 (2): 305–319.

Schubert, S. (2012b), "Is Coherence Conducive to Reliability?", Synthese, 187 (2): 607–621.

Schubert, S., and Olsson, E. J. (2013), "Coherence and Reliability in Judicial Reasoning," in Coherence: Insights from Philosophy, Jurisprudence and Artificial Intelligence, M. Araszkiewicz and J. Savelka (eds.), Law and Philosophy Library 107, Springer, pp. 33–58.

Schupbach, J. N. (2008), "On the Alleged Impossibility of Bayesian Coherentism," Philosophical Studies, 141 (3): 323–331.

Schupbach, J. N. (2011), "New Hope for Shogenji's Coherence Measure," British Journal for the Philosophy of Science, 62 (1): 125–142.

Shogenji, T. (1999), "Is Coherence Truth-Conducive?," Analysis, 59 (4): 338–345.

Shogenji, T. (2007), "Why Does Coherence Appear Truth-Conducive," Synthese, 157 (3): 361–372.

Shogenji, T. (2012), "The Degree of Epistemic Justification and the Conjunction Fallacy," Synthese, 184 (1), 29–48.

Shogenji, T. (2013), "Coherence of the Contents and the Transmission of Probabilistic Support," Synthese, 190 (13): 2525–2545.

Siebel, M. (2004), "On Fitelson's Measure of Coherence," Analysis, 64 (2): 189–190.

Siebel, M., and Wolff, W. (2008), "Equivalent Testimonies as a Touchstone of Coherence," Synthese 161 (2), 167–182.

Sosa, E. (1980), "The Raft and the Pyramid: Coherence Versus Foundations in the Theory of Knowledge," Midwest Studies in Philosophy, 5 (1): 3–26.

Thagard, P. (1989), "Explanatory Coherence," Behavioral and Brain Sciences 12 (3): 435–467.

Thagard (2000), Coherence in Thought and Action, Cambridge, MA: The Massachusetts Institute of Technology Press.

Weinberg, J. M., Nischols, S., and Stich, S. (2001), "Normativity and Epistemic Intuitions," Philosophical Topics 29 (1–2): 429–460.

Cambridge Elements ≡

Epistemology

Stephen Hetherington
University of New South Wales, Sydney

Stephen Hetherington is Professor Emeritus of Philosophy at the University of New South Wales, Sydney. He is the author of numerous books, including Knowledge and the Gettier Problem (Cambridge University Press, 2016) and What Is Epistemology? (Polity, 2019), and is the editor of several others, including Knowledge in Contemporary Epistemology (with Markos Valaris: Bloomsbury, 2019) and What the Ancients Offer to Contemporary Epistemology (with Nicholas D. Smith: Routledge, 2020). He was the Editor-in-Chief of the Australasian Journal of Philosophy from 2013 until 2022.

About the Series
This Elements series seeks to cover all aspects of a rapidly evolving field including emerging and evolving topics such as these: fallibilism; knowing-how; self-knowledge; knowledge of morality; knowledge and injustice; formal epistemology; knowledge and religion; scientific knowledge; collective epistemology; applied epistemology; virtue epistemology; wisdom. The series will demonstrate the liveliness and diversity of the field, pointing also to new areas of investigation.

Cambridge Elements ≡

Epistemology

Elements in the Series

Foundationalism
Richard Fumerton

The Epistemic Consequences of Paradox
Bryan Frances

Coherentism
Erik J. Olsson

The A Priori *Without Magic*
Jared Warren

A full series listing is available at: www.cambridge.org/EEPI